HERBS

Cultivating & Cuisine

by

Carol Asher

McClanahan
Publishing House

International Standard Book Number 0-913383 75 9
Library of Congress Catalog Card Number 00-112048

Cover design and book layout by James Asher Graphics
Illustrations by James Asher

Manufactured in the United States of America

All book order correspondence should be addressed to:

McClanahan Publishing House, Inc.
P.O. Box 100
Kuttawa, KY 42055
270-388-9388
1-800-544-6959
www.kybooks.com

FROM THE
HERB GARDEN
TO THE DINING TABLE

Adam, like any good gardener, surely must have ventured to the edge of Eden and looked out at the desolation beyond and thought, "So much to do and so much time." Now, here was a gardener with a lot of space for plants and a lot of time on his hands to plant anything he desired. A gardener's dream!

It has been said, "The measure of time began in a garden." There is a lot of truth in this statement when you think about the histories of the ingredients it takes to make a garden. Simply look at a garden, any garden. You will quickly see the structures making up the boundaries, then you will spot the plantings. Maybe you can envision the thinking behind the placement in this or that spot. Look a little closer and you will discover the personality of the gardener.

Everything has a history, including our surroundings. All of the items we see have pasts. There is history here.

In our herb garden, Cornerstone Gardens, my husband, Jim and I have brought together a culmination of time, energy and love. We uncovered stones buried about a foot deep in the garden area, which when we removed the dirt and looked at how they were laid out, we realized were hearthstones, probably from the mid to late 1800s. We base this on a dime. Literally two half-dimes we found from 1852 in this same location. The hearthstones became stepping stones leading into our gardens. We have tried to imagine the cabin and the people who lived there using the fireplace for cooking, warming, drying, or perhaps reading around what are now our steps.

We have also brought into our garden several cornerstones giving our garden its name. These stones originally provided a strong foundation for Jim's childhood home. They were most likely gathered from the woods and fields, which contain a lot of rock, and were then hewn into the needed shapes.

Included in our garden are many herbs with pedigrees that reach back into pre-history. The more plants we bring in, the more "pasts" we admit to our home. In working with herbs, I have always been intrigued with their histories. Learning more about the herb, such as where the lore surrounding the plant originated, where the plant originated, and who first recognized the many, many uses of herbs, I find intriguing.

By bringing together the hearthstones, the cornerstones, the herbs and all the histories to join in one garden, we are adding to their combined history. We moved the stones and gave them a new purpose. We cultivate herbs and bring them to our dining table as new and exciting tastes to experience. It's all history in the making.

Culinary use of herbs is never boring and always exciting. Finding new ways of using the herbs together to elicit a new flavor is a creative outlet. Cooking with herbs gives your family or guests a wonderful and healthy meal obtaining flavor from herbs and not salt.

Recipes containing herbs are easy to do year round. Harvesting herbs for cooking when they are fresh is, of course, ideal. But in some areas, fresh herbs are not as easy to find in the garden in winter. We can dry, freeze, prepare vinegars, or otherwise "put up" the herbs from our herb beds in preparation for winter cooking. Putting your herbs to good use in this way is a compliment to all the hard work you have put into your garden all summer. If you choose not to store your own herbs or do not garden with herbs but do appreciate cooking with them, many fresh herbs can readily be found in the produce section at the supermarket or as dried herbs in the baking aisle.

On a lighter side, I believe if you promise me herbs to garden and cook with, I'll easily find happiness. I know there is a history here, but like Adam, I look out over the gardens and I dream of so, so much to do, but unlike Adam, realize there is so, so little time!

Lamb's Ears

Contents

For my valiant daughter,
Terri Shawn

Coneflowers

Herbs bring a peace
grounding us to the earth —
permitting nature to be our mentor.
    Carol Asher

Appetizers

These stepping stones were uncovered while digging in our herb garden. We believe them to be the hearthstones from a long forgotten cabin.

HERBS

The old hearthstone steps speak to the history of our gardens and serve as a clear counterpoint to the formal layout of the herb garden beyond.

Bruschetta

If you have never been to a restaurant where they graced your table with fresh bread and a saucer of peppered olive oil, you are missing what ancient Romans shared after harvesting olives and presenting the first pressing. This tradition was probably the beginning of bruschetta which we would call "toasted bread."

Basically, preparing bruschetta consists of toasting bread, preferably over an open fire or grill, rubbing with raw garlic and topping with any combination of olive oil, tomatoes, garlic, and any selection of herbs or other toppers. The combination should be simple and served quickly after toasting and spreading the ingredients on top. This is a hearty appetizer or accompaniment to soups or salads.

Bruschetta with Basil

3 tomatoes, peeled, chopped, and seeded
1 clove garlic, minced
1 cup fresh basil, chopped
2 Tbsp. olive oil
1 loaf Italian bread
Parmesan cheese

Garlic

Combine the tomatoes, garlic, basil and olive oil in a glass bowl; let stand for 30 minutes. Cut bread into slices and grill or toast lightly under the broiler. Rub the toast with raw garlic and spoon tomato mixture over the toasted bread and sprinkle generously with Parmesan cheese. Serve immediately.

Grecian Bruschetta

Italian bread, thickly sliced
Olive oil
Fresh garlic
Tomatoes
Pitted ripe olives, chopped
Basil or oregano, chopped
Black pepper, freshly ground

Toast bread quickly over a grill or open fire. Brush with olive oil and rub with garlic. Grate tomatoes using the large holes of a hand-held grater so you can gather the pulp without juices and skin. Spread lavishly over the bread. Add ripe olives and herbs of choice. Add pepper to olive oil and drizzle over prepared bruschetta. Serve immediately.

Herbed Bruschetta

½ cup fresh Italian parsley, finely chopped
⅓ cup pitted ripe olives, chopped
1 Tbsp. fresh tarragon, minced
Freshly ground black pepper
¼ cup extra-virgin olive oil
2 large tomatoes
1 loaf French bread, thickly sliced

In a medium-size bowl, place the parsley, olives, tarragon, and pepper to taste. Add the oil and toss well. Dice the tomatoes and let come to room temperature. Toast or grill the bread and spread with the herb mixture. Top off with the tomato. Serve quickly.

Bruschetta with Tarragon Vinegar

1 large red tomato, halved and seeded
1 large yellow tomato, halved and seeded
2 Tbsp. olive oil
1 Tbsp. tarragon vinegar
1 clove garlic
¼ tsp. salt
Fresh ground pepper
Loaf Italian bread
Fresh basil leaves, julienned

Cut tomatoes into chunks. In a bowl, combine tomatoes, olive oil, and vinegar. Crush garlic, adding it to the mixture. Add salt. Let stand 15 minutes. Toast thick slices of the bread. Rub toast with raw garlic. Season the tomato mixture with a generous grinding of pepper. Spoon mixture over warm toast. Sprinkle with julienned fresh basil leaves. Serve immediately.

Hummingbird Garden
(Annual)

Salvia
Cleome
Scarlet Runner
Nicotiana
Nasturtium
Campanula
Catnip
Foxglove
Sage, Mexican
Monarda
Pineapple sage

Boursin (Cheese Spreads)

Cheese spreads, including boursin, can be easily prepared ahead of time. These spreads require few ingredients and by simply adding fresh herbs, they will delight your guests when they detect the unexpected flavor.

Create an attractive party platter by spreading onto a variety of breads and serve as open-faced sandwiches, topping off with an herb sprig on top. Spread on crackers or cherry or Roma tomato halves. Don't limit its use to appetizers. During meals spoon onto baked potatoes, or stir into mashed potatoes, and even spread on chicken while it's baking.

Garlicky Boursin

16 oz. cream cheese, softened
¼ cup mayonnaise
2 tsp. Dijon-style mustard
2 Tbsp. fresh chives, finely chopped
2 Tbsp. fresh dill, finely chopped
1 clove garlic, minced

Thoroughly blend all ingredients in a medium-size bowl with mixer or processor. Line a small bowl with tin foil and spoon in mixture. Cover; refrigerate overnight. Turn out onto a small serving plate and peel off foil. Serve with crackers for spreading. Can refrigerate for up to 4 days before serving.

Boursin Cheese Spread

Biennial
Herbs

Caraway
Chervil
Mullien
Parsley
Sage, Clary

1 clove garlic, minced
16 oz. cream cheese, softened
1 cup butter or margarine, softened
1 Tbsp. fresh oregano, chopped
1 Tbsp. fresh dill, chopped
1 Tbsp. fresh basil, chopped
1 Tbsp. fresh thyme, chopped
¼ tsp. pepper
½ tsp. Worcestershire sauce

Combine all ingredients, mix gently and thoroughly. Cover and refrigerate. Bring to room temperature prior to serving.

Tangy Chives & Dill Boursin

16 oz. cream cheese, softened
3 Tbsp. milk
1 large clove garlic, minced
¼ cup fresh dill
¼ tsp. fresh pepper
2 Tbsp. fresh chives, chopped
1 tsp. fresh chervil
6 drops hot sauce
Chopped chives for garnish

Chervil

Mix all ingredients until thoroughly blended. Line a bowl with plastic wrap leaving excess wrap around the edges. Spoon the cheese into the bowl and fold ends of wrap over the top. Refrigerate overnight. When ready to serve, turn out of the bowl, removing the wrap and top with the chopped chives.

Herbed Boursin

2 cloves garlic, minced
¼ cup fresh chives, chopped
¼ cup fresh parsley, chopped
¼ cup fresh basil, chopped
8 oz. cream cheese
¼ cup pitted black olives, chopped
French bread

Combine garlic and herbs, mixing thoroughly. Blend in the cream cheese until smooth. Add the olives. Place in a small bowl and garnish with basil leaves. Chill.

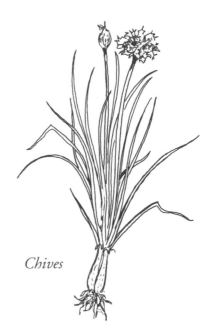

Chives

Herbed Walnuts

2 Tbsp. butter, melted
2 Tbsp. olive oil
1 lb. walnut halves
1½ Tbsp. dried rosemary, crushed (can substitute sage)
or 5 Tbsp. fresh, finely chopped herb
1 tsp. paprika
2 tsp. salt

Preheat oven to 325°. Combine melted butter and olive oil. Drizzle onto cookie sheet. Scatter nuts onto pan and stir. Spread out to a single layer. Sprinkle rosemary, paprika, and salt over nuts. Bake 20-25 minutes stirring several times or until golden brown. Drain on paper towels. Serve warm.

Hot Cream Cheese & Crab Spread

Thyme

8 oz. pkg. cream cheese, softened
6 oz. pkg. frozen crab meat, thawed, drained
(reserve 2 tablespoons liquid) and chopped
4 Tbsp. chives, snipped
1 tsp. lemon juice
1 tsp. lemon thyme
½ tsp. hot pepper sauce
⅓ cup sliced almonds
Bread rounds or crackers

In small bowl of mixer or processor mix thoroughly: cheese, reserved crab liquid, chives, lemon juice, thyme, and pepper sauce. Stir in crab meat. Turn into greased, shallow 3-cup baking dish. Sprinkle with almonds. Bake uncovered in pre-heated 350° oven 20-30 minutes or until bubbly. Serve hot as a spread on bread rounds. Makes 30-40 appetizers.

Fine herbes is a French term and simply means "finely chopped herbs." Chop and mix equal parts of parsley, chervil, chives, and French tarragon. Add to food during the final 15 minutes of cooking.

Cucumber Cheese Spread

2 large cucumbers, peeled and seeded, shredded and
drained
4 slices bacon, cooked and crumbled
¼ cup walnut chips
1 tsp. lemon juice
1 Tbsp. dill, minced
8 oz. cream cheese, softened
Celery seed
Salt & pepper to taste

Combine all ingredients and keep refrigerated. Serve on
bread or crackers. Makes 2 cups.

Layered Parmesan Cheese

16 oz. cream cheese, softened
2 tsp. lemon juice
⅓ cup Parmesan cheese, grated
1 Tbsp. chili sauce
½ cup cream-style cottage cheese, drained
⅛ cup chives, minced
1 small clove garlic, minced
½ cup fresh parsley, snipped

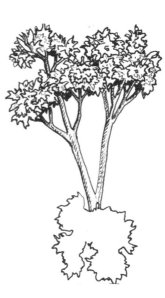

Parsley

In medium-size bowl, cream together cream cheese and
lemon juice until fluffy. Divide into two portions. To one
portion, stir in Parmesan and chili sauce. Turn into lightly
oiled 3 cup mold or bowl. To remaining cream cheese, add
cottage cheese, chives, and garlic. Beat until nearly smooth.
Stir in parsley. Spoon atop first layer in mold. Cover and
chill. Unmold. Makes about 2½ cups.

Beer Cheese Spread

2 cups shredded Cheddar cheese
3 oz. cream cheese, softened
2 Tbsp. minced fresh parsley
1 clove garlic, crushed
½ tsp. hot pepper sauce
⅓ cup beer

In small bowl, mix all ingredients, mixing in only enough beer to give a good spreading consistency. Cover and chill several hours. For easier spreading, remove from refrigerator half hour before serving. Use as a spread on assorted breads and crackers. Makes 1½ cups.

Garlic

Dawn's Quick & Easy Cheeseball

16 oz. cream cheese, softened
1 small pkg. Cheddar cheese, finely shredded
1 small onion, diced
1 small green pepper, diced
1 clove garlic, minced
1 tsp. fresh parsley, minced
1 small pkg. sandwich ham, finely chopped
Pecan pieces

Combine all ingredients and form into a ball. Roll in pecan pieces.

Dill Dip

1 tsp. dry mustard
1 Tbsp. lemon juice
1 cup mayonnaise
1 cup sour cream
2 Tbsp. dillweed, chopped
Salt to taste

Combine first 2 ingredients and stir until smooth. Add all other ingredients and mix well. Serve with seafood or raw vegetables. Makes 2 cups.

Spicy Cilantro Dip

3-oz. can pitted black olives, chopped
2 oz. green chiles, chopped
1 medium onion, chopped
1 large tomato, chopped
¼ cup cilantro chopped
1½ Tbsp. vinegar
3 Tbsp. olive oil
1 tsp. garlic powder

Combine all ingredients and chill for 2 hours prior to serving. Serve with corn chips. Makes 2½ cups.

Cilantro

Horseradish Dip

1 cup mayonnaise
1 cup sour cream
6 slices bacon, cooked and crumbled
¼ cup prepared horseradish

Horseradish

Combine ingredients thoroughly and cover. Chill. Approximately 2 cups.

Cody's Artichoke Dip

1 small can artichoke hearts, drained and minced
1 cup mayonnaise
1 cup Parmesan cheese, grated
2 cloves garlic, minced
2 tsp. fresh parsley, chopped

Combine all ingredients and bake at 350° for 45 minutes. Serve warm.

Moth Repellent
Equal parts of camphor, basil, lavender, rosemary and southernwood.

Cucumber Tea Sandwiches

Thinly sliced white bread, cut into small squares
Cream cheese, softened
Thin slices of cucumber, peeled
Salad Burnet

Slice and shape bread into desired sizes and lightly spread
with soft cream cheese. Top with thin slices of cucumber and
garnish with Salad Burnet leaves and blossoms.

*Salad
Burnet*

Herbed Potato Skins

3 baking potatoes
Vegetable oil
4 oz. Cheddar cheese, shredded
2 Tbsp. chives, chopped
1 tsp. thyme, minced
6 slices bacon, cooked and crumbled
Sour cream

Wash potatoes thoroughly, scrubbing and removing
blemishes with a knife. Rub skin with oil. Bake
for 1 hour in a 400° oven or until done. Allow potatoes
to cool. Cut in half and scoop out pulp, leaving ¼ inch
shell. Cut shells in half crosswise and deep fry in hot oil
for 2 minutes or until lightly browned. Drain on paper
towels. Place skins on a baking dish.

Combine cheese, herbs, and bacon. Sprinkle onto skins.
Place under broiler until cheese melts. Serve with sour
cream. Makes 12.

> No occupation is so
> delightful to me as the
> culture of the earth and
> no culture comparable
> to that of the garden.
>
> Thomas Jefferson, 1811

Toasty Cheese Rounds

¼ cup Mozzarella cheese, grated
¼ cup Parmesan cheese, grated
⅓ cup Romano cheese, grated
⅓ cup basil, chopped
¾ cup mayonnaise
½ cup red onion, chopped
1 loaf party rye bread

Mix the cheeses, basil, mayonnaise and onion. Spread on rye rounds. Broil until bubbly. Keep warm on hot tray. Serves 4 to 6.

Garlic Pecans

1 Tbsp. butter
3 Tbsp. soy sauce
2 tsp. hot pepper sauce
3 garlic cloves, mashed
1 lb. pecan halves
4 tsp. seasoned pepper
¼ tsp. dried red pepper flakes
Salt

Preheat oven to 350°. Coat baking sheet with 1 tablespoon butter. Sprinkle with soy sauce, hot pepper sauce and garlic. Scatter pecans over sheet and stir with fork until well coated. Sprinkle with 1½ teaspoons seasoned pepper, dried pepper flakes and salt. Bake 10 minutes. Sprinkle pecans with remaining seasoned pepper and additional salt if desired. Stir with fork. Bake 15 minutes. Cool before serving. Can be stored in jar for up to 3 months.

Perennial Herbs

Angelica
Artemisia
Bergamot
Catnip
Chamomile, Roman
Chives
Comfrey
Fennel
Feverfew
Germander
Horehound
Hyssop
Lavender
Lamon balm
Lovage
Marjoram
Mints
Mugwort
Oregano
Rosemary
Rue
Sage
Savory, winter
Sorrel
Southernwood
Sweet cicely
Tansy
Tarragon
Thyme
Wormwood
Yarrow

Rosemary Date Bites

½ cup butter or margarine, softened
1 cup Cheddar cheese, finely shredded
1½ cups all-purpose flour
1 Tbsp. fresh rosemary, finely minced
⅛ tsp. red pepper
Dash of paprika
25 pitted dates (about 6 oz.)

Combine butter and cheese; beat until smooth. Combine next four ingredients. Add to cheese mixture; mix well. Cut dates in half crosswise; wrap each half with dough. Place on ungreased baking sheets; bake at 400° for 15-18 minutes. Cool on wire racks. Makes approximately 50.

Rosemary

Pesto Stuffed Cherry Tomatoes

1 pt. cherry tomatoes
3-oz. pkg. cream cheese, softened
2 Tbsp. lemon juice
¼ cup freshly grated Parmesan cheese
¼ cup pine nuts, finely chopped
½ cup parsley, finely chopped
½ cup basil, finely chopped
2 cloves garlic, finely chopped

Cut tops off cherry tomatoes; scoop out pulp. Combine cream cheese with lemon juice in medium-size bowl until smooth. Stir in Parmesan, nuts, parsley, basil, and garlic. Fill cherry tomatoes with mixture and chill. Makes approximately 12.

Tisanes (teas)

The main garden consists of basic cooking herbs, while the flowering herb bed satisfies my desire for color.

My garden evolves a little each year giving me freedom to try new herbs.

The trellis arch is covered with grape vines, a favorite spot for children and birds.

The plum grove dining area is where I do some shade gardening with herbs.

$\mathcal{T}$ea is probably the most internationally known drink. It has been grown for centuries the world over. India and China are the biggest producers of tea today; however, the Chinese claim the earliest usage of tea for drinking, going back as much as 5,000 years ago.

Legend tells it was accidentally discovered by Chinese Emperor Shen Nung, who drank boiled water in which a tea leaf had blown through the window and into the water. Prior to this, tea was tossed into soups for extra flavoring. Formal tea-making came after Chinese potters invented the teapot. When this occurred, tea was on its way to becoming the most popular drink in the world.

Wars have been fought over tea. Remember the Boston Tea Party? Shipments of tea from Great Britain were thrown into the waters of the harbor and thus began the Revolutionary War. When the tea was not available to the citizens of the new world, they began looking around for a substitute. Herbal teas filled this billing. Already being used medicinally, herbs were a natural solution to their afternoon "teas".

Basically, there are four types of tea: Green tea, White tea, Oolong tea, and Black tea. The green teas are "unfermented" meaning they are not oxidized. The white teas (a sweeter tea) are air-dried and partially oxidized or fermented. They are picked prior to the leaf buds opening and still have their white hairs. Oolong teas are partially oxidized to stop the enzymatic action. This creates a milder flavor. The black tea, which we are so familiar with are fully oxidized with a stronger flavor than the others. The drying or oxidization process allows the tea leaves to become soft and fragrant. The leaves are tossed which bruises the edges and releases the enzymes that will oxidize the tea.

Herbal teas are green teas, which use fresh leaves that give health benefits to the drinkers. Herbal teas are flavorful and easy to prepare straight from your own garden.

When making teas, be careful not to use any plant you cannot identify with certainty. To be safe, plant a tea garden using: angelica, anise (seeds), basils (garden and lemon), bee balm (Oswego tea), borage, calendula, caraway, catmint, catnip, chamomile, dill (seeds), fennel (seeds), garden sage, ginger, horehound, lemon balm, lemon verbena, lovage, mints (not Pennyroyal), rosehips, rosemary, scented geraniums, sweet marjoram, thymes, yarrow.

Fresh Mint Tea

3 cups boiling water
8 tea bags
2 cups fresh mint leaves, bruised
2 cups sugar
¼ cup lemon juice (optional)
5 cups water

Pour boiling water over tea bags. Let steep for 10 minutes. Combine mint leaves, sugar and lemon juice with 5 cups water in a medium saucepan. Cook over medium heat, stirring frequently until sugar dissolves. Remove from heat. Let cool. Pour mixture through a seive into a serving pitcher. Add tea, stirring well. Serve over ice cubes. Makes 6-8 servings.

Mint

Herbal Tea

To make herbal teas, use:
    2 Tbsp. fresh herbs
      or 1 Tbsp. dried herb per cup.
    Add boiling water, cover and allow to steep at least 5 minutes.
    Strain into a cup.
    Add honey, sugar or cream to taste.
    Add a citrus slice or an herb for garnish.

Ginger Tea

Pour 1 pint of boiling water over 1 ounce of ginger rhizome. Steep for 5 to 20 minutes. Drink it hot or warm.

Note: On a cold winter's day, prepare a warm and invigorating tea with ginger.

Ginger

Lemon Herb Sun Tea

Tea leaves
Quart jar
Lemon herb leaves
Water

On a hot, sunny day, put one tablespoon of loose tea leaves in a quart jar. Add 3-4 springs lemon herb leaves (your choice: lemon balm, lemon thyme, lemon basil). Fill with water, cover, and set in the sun. When the tea has become a rich, amber color, place the jar in the refrigerator to cool. Strain. Add ice and garnish with fresh herb leaves. Makes 4 servings.

Drought Tolerant Herbs

Artemesia
Borage
Chamomile
Chives
Fennel
Feverfew
Geranium
Germander
Lamb's Ears
Lavender
Marjoram
Pennyroyal
Salad Burnet
Tansy
Thyme
Yucca

Lemon & Mint Tea

2 cups water

6 black tea bags

3 lemons, cut in to ½-inch thick slices

½ cup lemon balm leaves, bruised

1 cup mint leaves, crushed

Two 46-oz. cans pineapple juice

4 cups water

1 cup sugar

1½ tsp. vanilla extract

1½ tsp. almond extract

Borage

Bring water to a boil and pour over tea bags. Add lemons, lemon balm, and mint; cover and let stand 20 minutes. Strain. Combine tea mixture and remaining ingredients. Serve with ice and garnish with lemon balm leaves or borage flowers. Makes about 3 quarts.

Herbal Ice Cubes

Place desired herb sprig or edible flowers in ice trays, add water and freeze. Serve with iced tea, lemonade, punches and iced water.

Salads
&
Soups

Height of hedges is a matter of choice. The taller the plant, the more intriguing the trip through the maze.

The maze is always a treat for adults and children alike. You can easily be "lost in gardening" with this design.

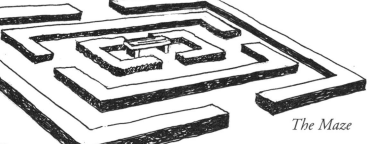

Mazes require a goal: a bench to rest, tower to climb, arch for roses, or a playhouse for children.

The Maze

Some aromatic and evergreen herbs to use: boxwood, germander, rue, winter savory, lavender, horehound, hyssop.

Summer Chicken Salad Mounds

8 oz. cooked chicken, finely chopped
⅓ cup water chestnuts, sliced and quartered
½ cup seedless grapes, halved
2 Tbsp. fresh basil
⅓ cup sliced almonds
Lettuce leaves
⅓ cup low-calorie mayonnaise
2 Tbsp. basil or white wine vinegar
1 Tbsp. soy sauce
1 tsp. curry powder
1 tsp. ground ginger
1 tsp. onion, grated
Walnuts

Basil

Combine chicken, water chestnuts, grapes, basil, and almonds in small bowl. Mound chicken salad in lettuce leaves on individual plates. With a whisk, stir together mayonnaise, vinegar, soy sauce, curry powder, ground ginger and onion. Pour dressing over chicken mounds. Surround mounds with fruits of choice. (Suggestions: bananas, pineapple chunks, sliced apples, strawberries, grapes, peaches, oranges). Sprinkle with walnuts. Serves 2.

Fennel is reputed to boost energy. Roman soldiers nibbled the seeds all day to stave off hunger on long marches; so did the Egyptian slaves who built the pyramids.

Tomatoes & Herb Vinaigrette Salad

½ cup fresh parsley
1 Tbsp. fresh tarragon
1 garlic clove
1 egg, room temperature
½ cup olive oil
¼ cup red basil vinegar
½ tsp. salt
Pepper, freshly ground
4 large tomatoes, cored and sliced
Bleu cheese, crumbled

Finely mince parsley, tarragon and garlic in food processor.
Add egg, oil, vinegar, salt and pepper and process 5 seconds
longer. Arrange tomato slices on cold serving platter. Pour
dressing over. Sprinkle with cheese.

On Valentine's day take two bay leaves sprinkled with rose water and
lay them over your pillow when you go to bed at night. You will dream
of your future spouse.

Minty Fruit Salad

1 medium Golden Delicious apple,
diced with peeling left on
1 medium Red Delicious apple, diced with peeling left on
½ cup seedless green grapes, halved
½ cup seedless red grapes, halved
1 small can pineapple chunks, drained
1 small can mandarin oranges, drained
½ cup sliced water chestnuts, halved

Topping:

2 oz. cream cheese, softened
¼ cup sour cream
¼ cup mayonnaise
¼ cup sugar
1 Tbsp. fresh mint, minced

Combine all fruits and water chestnuts in a large bowl. In a mixing bowl or processor, beat topping ingredients until smooth. Pour over fruit and toss gently. Serves 6.

Edible Herb Flowers

Anise hyssop (florets & flowers)
Bergamot (petals)
Borage (flowers)
Chives (florets & flowers)
Cresses (flowers)
Dill (florets)
Fennel, Bronze (flowers)
English Lavender (florets)
Garlic Chives
Mints
   (excluding pennyroyal)
   (florets & flowers)
Nasturtium (flowers)
Oregano (flowers)
Pansy (flowers)
Pineapple Sage (flowers)
Roses (petals)
Rosemary (flowers)
Sage officinalis (flowers)
Thyme (flowers)
Viola odorata (flowers)

Broccoli Salad with Lemon Thyme

4 cups broccoli florets
8 slices bacon
¾ cup mayonnaise
¼ cup sugar
1 tsp. fresh lemon thyme, minced
2 Tbsp. basil vinegar
3 scallions, finely chopped
Sliced water chestnuts, halved

Thyme

Cut up broccoli florets. Cook bacon, drain and cool, then break into bits. In a small bowl, mix mayonnaise, sugar, thyme, vinegar, scallions, and water chestnuts. Pour over broccoli florets and mix. Refrigerate until chilled.

Herb Marinated Cucumbers

2 small cucumbers, peeled and sliced
1 small can crabmeat, broken up
¼ cup chopped parsley
¼ cup dillweed, chopped
½ cup white vinegar
½ tsp. salt
1 tsp. sugar
Freshly ground black pepper

Combine all ingredients in medium bowl. Refrigerate several hours or overnight. Makes about 4½ cups.

Moisture Tolerant Herbs

Angelica
Bergamot
Chervil
Chives
Comfrey
Lady's mantle
Lovage
Mints
Parsley
Valerian
Violets

Marinated Herb Tomato Salad

6 tomatoes, cut into wedges
1 sweet red bell pepper, cut into strips
1 green bell pepper, cut into strips
1 medium purple onion, sliced and separated into rings
½ cup olive oil
¼ cup white wine vinegar
¼ cup chopped fresh parsley
2 cloves garlic, finely minced
½ cup scallions, chopped
1 tsp. fresh basil, minced
½ tsp. fresh oregano
½ tsp. salt
Freshly ground black pepper
Lettuce leaves

Place first 4 ingredients in a 13 x 9 x 2-inch dish and set aside. Combine next 9 ingredients in a jar; cover tightly and shake vigorously. Drizzle over vegetables; toss gently. Cover and chill at least 3 hours. Line a platter with lettuce leaves and drain vegetables, reserving liquid. Arrange on lettuce leaves. Drizzle with excess liquid and serve immediately. Serves 8.

Shade Tolerant Herbs

Angelica
Chervil
Chives
Comfrey
Fennel
Lemon balm
Mints
Parsley
Sweet woodruff
Tarragon, French
Thyme, lemon

Seven Layer Salad with Dill & Olives

1 cup broccoli florets, chopped
1 cup celery, chopped
1 cup scallions, chopped
1 pkg. frozen green peas, thawed and drained
1 cup mayonnaise
⅓ cup fresh dillweed, loosely packed
1 pkg. Cheddar cheese, grated
6 strips bacon, fried crisp and crumbled
Black olives

Place alternating layers of vegetables in bowl in order listed;
spread mixture of mayonnaise and dillweed over the top.
Cover with cheese and bacon. Sprinkle olives on top. Store
in refrigerator. Will keep for 1 week.

Dill

Spinach Salad with Pomegranate Seeds

1 lb. spinach, trimmed, well washed and torn
4 Tbsp. olive oil
3 Tbsp. fresh chives
¼ cup red basil vinegar
Salt
Pepper, freshly ground
½ cup pomegranate seeds

Into a large bowl place torn spinach. Set aside. Mix olive oil,
chives, vinegar, salt and pepper with a whisk. Pour over the
spinach and toss, mixing well. Place on salad plates and garnish with pomegranate seeds. Makes 4 servings.

German Hot Potato Salad

2 lbs. small white potatoes
1 tsp. salt
½ cup diced bacon
½ cup onion, minced
1½ tsp. all-purpose flour
4 tsp. sugar
1 Tbsp. salt
¼ tsp. pepper
⅓ cup tarragon or wine vinegar
½ cup water
¼ cup onion, minced
¼ cup chives, chopped
2 Tbsp. parsley, snipped
1 tsp. celery seeds
Parsley leaves

Everlastings

Baby's Breath
Celosia
Chinese Lantern
Cockscomb
Globe Ameranth
Globe Thistle
Honesty
Lavenders
Ornamental grasses
Poppy pods
Statice
Strawflower
Tansy

In 1-inch boiling water, cook potatoes in jackets, with salt added and covered with a lid. Cook until fork tender, about 35 minutes. Drain; peel; cut into ¼-inch slices. In small skillet, fry bacon until crisp. Add ½ cup minced onion; sauté until just tender, not brown. Meanwhile, in bowl mix flour, sugar, 1 tablespoon salt, and pepper. Stir in vinegar and water until smooth. Add to bacon; simmer, stirring until slightly thickened. Pour this hot dressing over potatoes. Add minced onion, chives, parsley, and celery seeds. Toss lightly; garnish with parsley leaves. Makes 4-6 servings.

Tuscan Bread Salad

4 cups day-old Italian bread, torn into bite-sized pieces
2 large tomatoes, seeded and coarsely chopped
1 green bell pepper, cut into chunks
1 small red onion, cut into slices and separated
1 small cucumber, peeled, seeded and sliced
½ cup fresh basil, chopped
2 Tbsp. fresh parsley, chopped
2 cloves garlic, minced
3 Tbsp. white wine vinegar
3 Tbsp. olive oil
¼ tsp. salt
¼ tsp. pepper
5 cups mixed greens, torn
Parmesan cheese, grated

Combine bread, tomatoes, bell pepper, red onion, cucumber, basil, parsley, and garlic in a large mixing bowl. To prepare the dressing, blend together vinegar, olive oil, salt, and pepper. Spoon over salad ingredients and toss gently. Let stand for 15 minutes to allow the flavors to blend. Serve over torn greens. Sprinkle with cheese. Approximately 6 servings.

Mesclun is the French Provençal term given to a mixture of tender young lettuce and greens served with just a simple dressing. Create your own mix of greens for a wonderful salad that is prepared in minutes. For a variation, wilt the greens with a small amount of hot oil and add to hot pasta. Sprinkle with grated cheese and ripe olives.

Tomato Cheese Salad with Chives

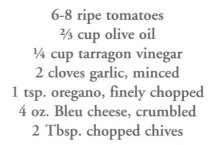

6-8 ripe tomatoes
⅔ cup olive oil
¼ cup tarragon vinegar
2 cloves garlic, minced
1 tsp. oregano, finely chopped
4 oz. Bleu cheese, crumbled
2 Tbsp. chopped chives

Thinly slice tomatoes into a shallow baking dish. Combine oil, vinegar, garlic, oregano and cheese in a 2-cup measure. Beat with fork to mix well; pour over tomatoes. Refrigerate several hours until well-chilled. Garnish with chives.

Chives

Bouquet Garni 1

1 clove garlic
1 Tbsp. dried parsley
2 tsp. dried basil
1 tsp. dried rosemary
1 tsp. dried oregano
2 bay leaves
6 whole peppercorns

Tie together in a cheesecloth bag. Add bag to soups and stews.

Tarragon Pork Stew

3 lbs. pork stew cubes
¼ cup flour
1 tsp. salt
½ tsp. freshly ground black pepper
Butter or margarine
1 cup water
1 rib celery, halved
½ cup dry white wine
1 bay leaf
2 Tbsp. fresh tarragon
5 potatoes, peeled and quartered
1 lb. small white onions

Coat meat with mixture of flour, salt and pepper. Brown a
few pork cubes at a time in 3 tablespoons hot butter in
Dutch oven, removing meat as it browns (add more butter if
necessary). Add water and stir to loosen brown bits.

Add meat and remaining ingredients, including any leftover
flour mixture. Cover and bake in 325° oven 2½ hours or
until meat and vegetables are fork tender. Skim off fat; discard bay leaf. Makes 6 servings.

Take a note: those styrofoam peanuts that fly
everywhere when you open a box can be used to
improve drainage in your large herb containers.

Herbed Potato Soup

2 large potatoes, diced
2-3 cups water
Pepper and salt to taste
4 Tbsp. butter or margarine, divided
1 medium onion, sliced
3 Tbsp. corn starch
2 cup milk
1 large can evaporated milk
Bacon, cooked and crumbled
4 Tbsp. chives, chopped

In a medium saucepan, cook potatoes in water until fork tender. Drain, reserving liquid. Add pepper and salt, and 1 tablespoon butter to drained potatoes. Set aside. In a large, heavy saucepan, melt 3 tablespoons butter over medium heat and add onions. Cook until tender; do not brown. Add 2 cups of reserved liquid to onions and cornstarch. Stir well. Cook until thickened, stirring constantly. Add 2 cups milk and potato mixture. Pour in evaporated milk. Gently reheat the soup. (Do not boil.) Ladle the soup into bowls and sprinkle with bacon and chives. Serves 6.

Revive the flavor of long-dried herbs by soaking them for 10 minutes in lemon juice or olive oil.

Quick Tomato Soup with Floating Basil Leaf

2 cans condensed tomato soup
¾ cup chicken broth
1 soup can of water
½ cup leftover mashed potatoes
1 Tbsp. fresh basil, finely minced
1 tsp. curry powder
Dash freshly ground black pepper

Combine all ingredients together with processor or rotary beater; heat. Serve with garnish of a floating basil leaf. Serves 4.

Herb Plants for Dye

Gold: Golden Marguerite, Marigold, Goldenrod
Green: Heather, white & pink flowered Yarrow, Stinging Nettle
Grey: Horsetail, Tansy
Orange: Coreopsis, Zinnia
Red: Madder, Marjoram, Rue, Henna, Coreopsis
Rust: Safflower, Zinnia
Scarlet: Yellow Bedstraw
Yellow: Catnip, Golden Marguerite, Heather, Tansy, Yellow Bedstraw, Coreopsis, Goldenrod, Safflower, Stinging Nettle

Sour Cream Cucumbers

3 medium cucumbers, peeled
1 large mild onion
Salt
Ice water
½ cup oil
½ cup vinegar
1 cup sour cream
Pepper
Minced parsley
1 tsp. chives, finely minced
Paprika
Salad Burnet for garnish

Parsley

Run tines of fork down cucumbers to score, then slice cucumbers and onions thinly. Alternating layers of cucumber and onion in bowl, sprinkle each layer with salt. Add ice water just to cover. Cover and chill several hours.

Drain in colander, rinsing well with cold running water; drain well. Return to bowl, add oil and vinegar and mix. Cover and marinate in refrigerator several hours. Drain, add sour cream and pepper and mix well. Stir in parsley, chives and paprika. Garnish with Salad Burnet. Makes 6-8 servings.

Herbs for a Moon Garden

Butterfly Bush, White Cloud
Coneflower, Alba
Cosmos, Purity
Dusty Miller, Silver Feather
Nicotiana, Shade Star
Sweet Alyssum
Zinnia, Star White

Gazpacho

2 jalapeño peppers, diced
1 tsp. hot sauce
2 Tbsp. fresh parsley, finely chopped
1 tsp. fresh cilantro, finely chopped
1 Tbsp. fresh basil, finely chopped
3 large tomatoes, peeled, seeded and finely chopped
1 cucumber, peeled, seeded and finely chopped
1 cup green pepper, finely chopped
½ cup onion, chopped
3 cups vegetable juice cocktail
Pepper and salt to taste
Sliced cucumber, freshly chopped basil or parsley to garnish

Combine all ingredients and chill at least 2 hours. Serve garnished with cucumber slices, freshly chopped basil or parsley. If you desire smooth soup, puree mixture 12 seconds in processor. Makes 6 cups.

Enter, solemnly tripping one after another, six personages clad in white robes, wearing on their heads garlands of Bays or Palms in their hands.

Shakespeare, from *Henry VIII*

Breads

Formula: 1. On your site, create a square. From the center point, draw a circle using string as a compass.

2. Divide each side of the square in half and draw an arch from corner to corner.

3. Connect each mid-point with straight lines to create the diamond.

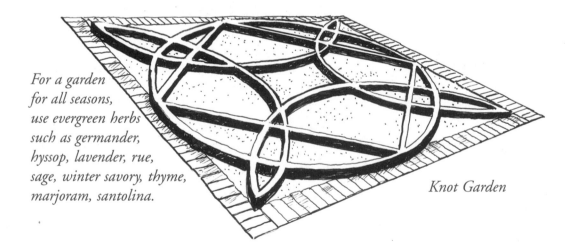

For a garden for all seasons, use evergreen herbs such as germander, hyssop, lavender, rue, sage, winter savory, thyme, marjoram, santolina.

Knot Garden

Knots are a challenge for any herb adventurist. Careful planning is required and a lot of patience, but the effect is well worth the effort.

Terri's Mexican Cornbread

1 lb. ground beef, browned
2 cups self-rising cornmeal
1 tsp. fresh cilantro, finely chopped
1 egg
Milk, enough to make pouring consistency
1 cup sharp cheese, shredded
1 onion, chopped
2 jalapeño peppers, chopped fine
15-oz. can corn, cream style

Brown and drain ground beef and set aside. Mix
cornmeal, cilantro, egg and milk, putting half into buttered
iron skillet. Add layer of each: ground beef, cheese, onion,
peppers, and corn. Then pour remaining cornbread
mixture on top. Bake at 350° until brown on top
and firm in the middle. Serves 8 to 10.

Orange Butter

¼ lb. butter
1 tsp. grated orange peel
2 Tbsp. orange juice
1 Tbsp. powdered sugar
¼ tsp. coriander

Soften butter to room
temperature. With electric
mixer at lowest speed, mix
all ingredients. Gradually
increase speed to high and
whip 8 to 10 minutes
until fluffy. Line mold
with plastic wrap. Press
butter into mold and
chill. Makes ½ cup.

Parmesan & Oregano Toast

2 Tbsp. olive oil
2 medium cloves garlic, minced
2 Tbsp. fresh oregano, chopped
1 loaf French or Italian bread, split lengthwise
3 Tbsp. grated Parmesan cheese

In a medium skillet, heat oil on medium to low heat. Add
garlic and cook until garlic releases its fragrance, about 1
minute. Stir in oregano. Drizzle the oil mix over cut sides of
bread. Sprinkle with cheese and broil 5-6 inches from broiler
for 1-3 minutes or until golden brown.

Basil & Thyme Buttermilk Biscuits

2 cups self-rising flour
1 tsp. sugar
¼ tsp. baking soda
⅓ cup shortening
3 Tbsp. butter
½ cup chopped basil
¼ cup chopped thyme
¾ cup buttermilk
Melted butter

In a large mixing bowl, stir flour, sugar, and baking soda together. Cut in shortening and butter until mixture resembles coarse crumbs. Stir in basil and thyme. Add buttermilk and mix well.

Turn dough out onto floured board and knead until smooth. Roll dough flat until approximately half inch thick. Cut with 2-inch cookie cutter. Place on lightly greased cookie sheet so they just touch each other. Brush tops with melted butter. Bake in a 425° oven for 15-18 minutes. Makes about 15 biscuits.

Fresh Green Onion Butter

½ cup butter
¼ cup fresh green onion, finely minced
1 Tbsp. fresh parsley, minced
1 tsp. freshly ground pepper
½ tsp. dry mustard

Combine all ingredients in a small mixing bowl, blending well. Serve with hot bread or baked potatoes. Makes ¾ cup.

Parmesan Rosemary Scones

1 cup flour
1 cup Parmesan cheese, grated
1 Tbsp. baking powder
½ tsp. salt
1 Tbsp. thyme, chopped
4 Tbsp. unsalted butter
2 Tbsp. extra-virgin olive oil
2 Tbsp. honey
1 egg
½ cup heavy cream
¼ cup rosemary, finely chopped
2 cloves garlic, crushed
Cayenne pepper, ground

In a large bowl, combine dry ingredients. With a fork, cut in butter until mixture resembles coarse meal. Stir in all other ingredients except cayenne pepper until dough holds together. Drop dough onto a lightly greased baking sheet about one-inch apart. Sprinkle with pepper. Bake in a preheated 400° oven 10-12 minutes or until golden. Makes approximately 8.

Rosemary Garlic Butter

½ cup butter, softened
1 clove garlic, crushed in a garlic press
2 Tbsp. fresh rosemary, finely chopped
½ tsp. parsley
1 tsp. lemon juice

Stir softened butter until fluffy. Add all other ingredients and mold as desired.

Tarragon Rolls

2¾ cups all-purpose flour, divided
1 pkg. active dry yeast
2 Tbsp. sugar
1 Tbsp. fresh parsley, minced
1 Tbsp. fresh tarragon, minced
or 1 tsp. dried tarragon
½ tsp. celery seed
½ tsp. salt
1 cup warm water
1 egg
2 Tbsp. oil
Butter

Tarragon

In a large mixing bowl, combine 1½ cups of flour, yeast, sugar, parsley, tarragon, celery seed and salt. Add water, egg and oil; beat on low speed for 30 seconds. Beat on high for 1 minute. Stir in remaining flour. Do not knead. Cover and let rise in a warm place until doubled, about 30 minutes. Stir dough and spoon into greased muffin cups. Cover and let rise in a warm place until doubled, about 20-30 minutes. Bake at 375° for 15 minutes. Brush with butter. Makes 18 rolls.

Tarragon Butter

½ cup unsalted butter,
room temperature
2 Tbsp. fresh tarragon,
minced (1-2 tsp. dried)
½ tsp. lemon juice

Combine all ingredients in small bowl and mix well. Mold. Makes ½ cup.

Herbed Yeast Rolls

1 pkg. dry yeast
2 cups warm milk
½ cup sugar
½ cup shortening
3½ to 4 cups self-rising flour
2-3 Tbsp. Herbs of choice

Dissolve yeast in milk. Add sugar, then shortening. Mix in flour and herbs of choice. Put in refrigerator. Pinch off and use as needed. Bake at 350°.

Herbs of Choice: basil, chives, rosemary, thyme, sage, dill, savory, parsley, oregano

Savory

Pepper & Chive Cornbread

1 cup self-rising cornmeal
½ cup self-rising flour
1 egg
⅓ cup chives, snipped
⅓ cup green pepper, chopped
1 cup buttermilk
1 Tbsp. butter

Combine all ingredients except butter. In a 400° oven, melt butter in an 8-inch black iron skillet or baking dish. Heat until butter is sizzling. Pour cornbread mix into skillet and bake 20 minutes or until golden brown on top. Turn out onto a plate.

Oregano Parmesan Clover Leaf Rolls

Oregano

1 cup milk, scalded
¼ cup shortening
1½ Tbsp. sugar
1 tsp. salt
1 cake yeast
1 Tbsp. lukewarm water
3 cups all-purpose flour, divided
1 egg, well beaten
½ cup fresh oregano, chopped
Melted butter
Parmesan cheese, grated

Scald milk, add shortening, sugar and salt. Cool to luke-warm. Crumble yeast and soften in lukewarm water, then add to lukewarm milk mixture. Add 1½ cup flour, beat until smooth. Add egg and stir well, then add oregano and remaining flour to make a moderately soft dough. Knead until smooth. Place in greased bowl, cover and let rise in a warm place until doubled in bulk. (About 1 hour.) Place 3 balls into each section of a greased muffin pan, brush with melted butter and sprinkle lavishly with Parmesan cheese. Cover and let rise until light. (About 30-45 minutes.) Bake in 400° oven 15-25 minutes. Makes about 24.

Parsley Butter

½ cup butter
¼ cup fresh parsley, minced
1 tsp. lemon juice
Freshly ground black pepper

Let butter soften slightly and cream with a fork. Add remaining ingredients and mix thoroughly. Makes ½ cup.

Basil Bread Slices

4 tsp. Parmesan cheese, freshly grated
4 tsp. fresh basil leaves, finely chopped
1 large clove garlic, peeled and minced
⅛ tsp. black pepper, freshly ground
16 ½-inch thick slices French or Italian bread
4 tsp. extra-virgin olive oil

In a small bowl, mix Parmesan, basil, garlic and pepper.
Arrange bread on a baking sheet and brush each slice with
olive oil. Spread mixture on bread. Broil 2-3 minutes, until
bread is lightly browned and crisp and bubbly. Serve hot.
Makes 16.

Cucumber Butter Spread

1 medium cucumber
½ cup butter, softened
8 oz. cream cheese, softened
1 clove garlic, minced

Wash and grate cucumber with peeling.
Set aside to drain. Combine butter,
cream cheese, and garlic. Add drained
cucumber. Mix well and shape. Chill.
Serve with crackers or party rye bread.
Make a dip simply by
not draining the cucumber.

Tomato & Garlic Loaf

¼ cup butter or margarine
6 medium tomatoes, coarsely chopped
3 medium onions, chopped
6 cloves garlic, finely chopped
½ cup fresh parsley, chopped
2 Tbsp. fresh oregano, chopped
1 tsp. salt
½ tsp. pepper
8-oz. pkg. Mozzarella cheese, shredded
½ cup freshly grated Parmesan cheese
1 loaf unsliced Italian bread

Melt butter in large skillet; add chopped tomatoes, onions, garlic, 2 tablespoons of the parsley, oregano, salt and pepper. Cook, stirring often, over high heat until sauce thickens and most of the liquid is evaporated, about 15 to 20 minutes. Combine cheeses with remaining parsley. Slice bread in half horizontally. Spread with tomato mixture. Top with cheese mix. Bake in 400° oven 15 minutes or until the cheese is golden brown and bubbly.

Garlic Butter

8 cloves garlic,
 finely chopped
1 cup butter, softened
½ tsp. red pepper
1 tsp. Worcestershire sauce
2 Tbsp. parsley, chopped
1 Tbsp. lemon juice

Blend all ingredients until creamy. Chill. Spread on French bread and wrap in foil. Cook over hot coals on the grill or heat in oven at 400°.

Herb & Cheese Crescent Loaf

8-oz. pkg. cream cheese, softened
1 Tbsp. fresh parsley flakes
1 Tbsp. fresh basil, chopped coarsley
1 Tbsp. fresh chives, snipped
½ tsp. dillseeds
¼ tsp. garlic powder
8-oz. can refrigerated crescent dinner rolls
1 egg, slightly beaten
½ tsp. poppy seeds

Basil

Combine first 6 ingredients in a small bowl; stir well. Set aside. Unroll crescent rolls into two rectangles; connect ends to make one long rectangle. Press perforations to seal. Spread cream cheese mixture over crescent rolls to within ½ inch of edge. Roll, starting at long side, jellyroll fashion. Pinch edges to seal.

Place on a lightly greased baking sheet. Using kitchen shears, cut ½ inch slices alternating from right to left side of dough, being careful not to cut completely through the dough. Pull out alternating sides, exposing jellyroll pattern. Brush with egg; sprinkle with poppy seeds. Bake at 375° for 12-15 minutes. Makes 6-8 servings.

Moth Repellent
2 cups each dried spearmint, dried peppermint, dried rosemary; 1 cup dried thyme; 1 cup southernwood; ½ cup ground cloves.

Entrées

The seventh-century Irish patron saint of gardeners, St. Fiacre stands sentinel over gardens encouraging them to be fruitful. An Irish prayer from gardeners to the saint tenderly says,
"St. Fiacre, opener of the world to the outpouring of Divine healing love through garden herbs and flowers."

Mandarin Pork Chops with Rosemary & Thyme

Four 1-inch pork chops
1 Tbsp. margarine
11-oz. can mandarin oranges
¼ cup brown sugar, firmly packed
½ tsp. ground cinnamon
½ tsp. ground cloves
1 tsp. salt
½ tsp. ground mustard
¼ cup tomato ketchup
1 Tbsp. basil or cider vinegar
1 medium green sweet pepper, cut into large pieces
2 stems fresh rosemary
½ tsp. dried thyme

*Rosemary &
Thyme*

Brown pork chops on both sides in margarine. Drain mandarin oranges, reserving juice. Set fruit aside and combine juice with remaining ingredients except rosemary and thyme. Pour over pork chops. Lay stems of rosemary on pork chops. Cover and simmer on low for 30-45 minutes or until pork chops are tender. Add thyme and oranges the last 10 minutes of cooking time. Serves 4.

Pesto

If you plan on making a lot of pesto for freezing, leave out both the garlic and nuts. Add them to the thawed pesto and blend together just before use. For variations of pesto, substitute other varieties of nuts instead of pine nuts. These can be walnuts, pecans, or almonds. The basil can be opal or lemon. Use your creativity to come up with your "own" pesto. Serve over noodles or rice.

Skillet Pork Chops

1 medium onion, sliced
2 cloves garlic, minced
3 Tbsp. oil
3 Tbsp. all-purpose flour
1 tsp. salt
½ tsp. pepper, freshly ground
Four 1-inch pork chops
16-oz. can tomatoes, with juice
1 bay leaf
14½-oz. can green beans, drained
2 Tbsp. basil, dried or fresh
1 Tbsp. oregano

Garlic

In a large skillet, sauté onion and garlic in oil until tender. Do not brown. Remove onion and garlic from skillet and set aside. Combine flour, salt and pepper. Dredge pork chops in flour mixture. Brown chops on both sides in skillet drippings. Add tomatoes, onion, and bay leaf; bring to a boil. Reduce heat, cover and simmer for 1½ hours. Add green beans, basil and oregano during the last 10 minutes. Remove bay leaf and serve in skillet. Serves 4.

Herbal Bath Water

Pour boiling water over herbs, then strain the water and put it in your bath or apply it as a refreshing facial splash.

Potatoes 'n Pork Chops

¼ cup oil
1 Tbsp. butter
1 small onion, sliced
2 cloves garlic, minced
Olive oil
3 large potatoes, peeled and sliced
Four 1-inch pork chops
Flour
½ cup chicken broth
½ tsp. fresh rosemary, minced
1 tsp. fresh thyme, chopped
Black pepper

Place oil and butter in large skillet. Cook onions and garlic until soft. Do not brown. Remove from skillet and reserve.

Add olive oil to skillet and sauté potatoes until tender over medium heat. Cover to speed cooking and turn often. Add to onion mixture and reserve.

Dredge pork chops in flour. Brown pork chops in skillet on both sides. Lower heat and return potato and onion mixture to pan. Add broth, rosemary, thyme and pepper to taste. Cover and simmer about 20 minutes or until pork chops are tender. Serve as a one-dish meal. Garnish with a rosemary sprig. Serves 4.

Butterfly Garden Herbs

(Annual)

Cosmos
Dianthus
Marigold
Zinnia

Chinese Pork Chops

6 pork chops, ½ inch thick
1 Tbsp. oil
½ cup granulated sugar
2 Tbsp. cornstarch
¼ cup vinegar
2 tsp. soy sauce
1 cup water
1 chicken-bouillon cube
1 Tbsp. Lemon Balm, chopped
8-oz. can crushed pineapple, undrained

Lemon Balm

Trim excess fat from pork chops. In oil, sauté chops until browned on both sides; remove chops and turn down heat. In small bowl thoroughly blend sugar and cornstarch; stir in vinegar, soy sauce, and water; add with bouillon cube, lemon balm and pineapple to skillet; simmer, stirring constantly, until thickened. Return chops to skillet; simmer, covered, over low heat, until chops are tender and no longer pink inside (30 to 45 minutes). Serve with pan gravy. Makes 6 servings.

Sweetleaf is an evergreen herb, easily grown and a natural sugar substitute. It has a minty appearance with white flowers resembling baby's breath. The leaves are edible by just pinching from the plant. Much sweeter than granulated sugar, the leaves can be dried and powdered to use as an additive to foods and drinks.

Broiled Ham Slices with Molasses Butter

¼ cup butter, softened
1 Tbsp. molasses
½ tsp. lemon juice
1 tsp. thyme, chopped
4 Tbsp. freshly ground black pepper
Salt to taste
4 pre-cooked ham slices

Stir together butter, molasses, lemon juice and thyme. Cover and refrigerate. Broil slices 6 inches from broiler for 3 minutes on each side. Upon last turn, sprinkle with thyme, pepper and salt. Top each slice with molasses butter and serve. Serves 4.

To prepare an herb butter, place ½ cup softened butter in a small bowl. Cream the butter until fluffy with a spoon or mixer. Stir in your choice of chopped or minced herbs. Place in a mold that has been lined with plastic wrap large enough to enclose all the butter; or, roll into a log, cover with plastic wrap. Chill. Can be frozen for up to 2 months.

French Omelette

3-4 eggs
1 Tbsp. water
Salt to taste
Pepper, fresh ground to taste
1½ Tbsp. margarine

Break eggs into bowl, adding water, salt, and pepper. Stir with a fork until blended but not frothy. Melt margarine in a 8-inch rounded-bottom skillet or omelette pan over medium heat. As it melts, coat the sides and bottom well with the melted margarine. The margarine will quickly foam. As soon the foaming ends, remove skillet from heat and pour in egg mixture. Return to heat. With the flat side of the fork, stir the eggs briskly in a circular motion as you shake the pan back and forth over the heat. Stir only until the eggs begin to set. Cook less than a minute. Shake the pan; the omelette should move freely. Add filling of choice to the center. Tilt the handle of the pan up; with the fork begin to roll the edge nearest the handle toward the center, rolling it approximately into thirds. Complete the rolling by tilting the omelette and dishing onto a warm plate. Serves 2.

Suggested fillings:

• Prepare 1 slice American cheese, cut in strips; ½ small tomato, seeded and chopped; ¼ tsp. fresh basil; 1 slice cooked bacon, crumbled. Fill center of omelette.

• Prepare shredded Cheddar or Swiss cheese; 1 tsp. chopped chives and place into center of omelette.

• Prepare minced tomato, peeled and seeded; salt and freshly

ground pepper to taste with a bit of dairy sour cream and a sprinkling of fresh or dried dill. Fill center of omelette.

• Add to eggs prior to cooking: 1 tsp. of each: chervil, chives and ½ tsp. of parsley leaves, all finely chopped. Sprinkle Parmesan cheese over top of omelette.

• Finely mince half an onion and cook with butter in an omelette pan, letting it brown slightly. Add the eggs with which a large pinch of chopped parsley has been mixed and cook the omelette.

• Sauté 1 cup hash-browned potatoes in 1 Tbsp. margarine. Add to center of omelette along with 1 Tbsp. chopped chives and 2 Tbsp. riced cream cheese.

• Stir chopped, seeded tomato and 1 tsp. oregano into egg mixture prior to cooking. Sprinkle with Parmesan cheese.

• Add finely chopped ham, shredded Swiss cheese and parsley. Serve with raisin sauce or warmed jellied cranberry sauce.

Rule of Thumb: Don't use more than three herbs in an omelette, using less of the strongest herb. The herbs may be added into the egg mixture prior to cooking or added to the filling. Be sure to have the filling ready prior to cooking the omelette.

For basting food, tie a few sprigs of flavorful herbs together and dip in basting sauce or butter. Some herbs to use are rosemary, thyme, and chervil.

Little Mary's Chicken Tetrazzini Casserole

1 fryer chicken
1 green pepper, chopped
1 medium onion, chopped
16-oz. box long spaghetti, broken
1 can cream of mushroom soup
⅛ cup fresh dill, minced
¼ tsp. black pepper, freshly ground
1 small can mushroom pieces
8 oz. American cheese, cut in small pieces

Stew chicken. Reserve cooking broth; remove skin and meat from bones, discarding skin. Cook pepper and onion in chicken broth until tender. Add spaghetti, mushroom soup, dill, black pepper, mushrooms, and liquid. Add cheese and stir over heat until cheese melts. Add chicken. Place in casserole dish. Bake covered in a 350° oven for 25 minutes. Makes 6-8 servings.

Lavender blue and rosemary green,
When I am king, you shall be queen.

Mother Goose

Chicken & Sage à la King

2 Tbsp. chopped green pepper
2 Tbsp. butter
1 can cream of mushroom soup
½ can green peas, drained
⅓ cup milk
1 cup cooked chicken, diced
2 Tbsp. pimento, diced
¼ cup fresh chives, minced
1 Tbsp. sage, rubbed
Biscuit halves, cooked

Sage

In saucepan, cook green pepper in butter until tender. Stir in soup until smooth. Add remaining ingredients. Cook over medium heat until heated through. Serve over biscuit halves. Makes approximately 4 servings.

Good Tip
If it simmers, it can take a bay leaf.
(Remove the leaf before serving.)

Sage Dumplings with Chicken

Sage

½ cup chicken broth
2 Tbsp. vegetable oil
1½ cups self-rising flour
2 Tbsp. fresh sage, finely chopped
2 qts. broth
Cooked chicken

Add ½ cup chicken broth and oil to the self-rising flour and sage, stirring until moistened. Turn dough out on a floured surface and form into a ball. Roll dough to 1/16-inch thickness; cut into 5x1-inch strips. Drop dumplings into boiling broth; cover and cook 15 minutes or until dumplings are tender. Add cooked chicken. Serves 8.

Now 'tis the spring, and weeds are shallow-rooted.
Suffer them now and they'll o'ergrow the garden.

William Shakespeare

Honey & Basil Chicken

1 cup red wine or basil vinegar
3 Tbsp. Dijon mustard
2 Tbsp. soy sauce
3 Tbsp. honey
3 Tbsp. fresh basil, chopped
¼ cup fresh thyme, chopped
Freshly ground black pepper
4 boneless, skinless chicken breast halves
Rice

Basil

In a shallow glass baking dish, mix the vinegar, mustard, soy sauce, honey, basil, thyme, and pepper. Add the chicken and turn to coat all sides. Marinate at room temperature for 15 minutes. Transfer the chicken to grill or broiling rack; reserve the marinade and place in a small saucepan. Grill or broil the chicken for 5 minutes on each side or until cooked through. While the chicken is cooking, boil the marinade until reduced by half. Pour marinade over chicken and serve with rice. Serves 4.

Herb Insect Repellents

Artemisia
Catnip
English Pennyroyal
Mint
Rue
Santolina
Southernwood
Tansy

Crockpot Lemon Chicken

Two 2½-3 lb. broiler-fryer chickens, cut up
¼ cup all-purpose flour
1¼ tsp. salt
2 Tbsp. cooking oil
6-oz. can frozen lemonade concentrate, thawed
3 Tbsp. brown sugar
3 Tbsp. catsup
1 Tbsp. vinegar
¼ cup fresh basil, chopped
1 Tbsp. rosemary, finely chopped
2 Tbsp. cold water
2 Tbsp. cornstarch
Hot cooked rice

Combine the flour with salt; coat chicken thoroughly. Brown chicken pieces on all sides in hot oil; drain. Transfer to a crock pot. Stir together the lemonade concentrate, brown sugar, catsup, vinegar, basil and rosemary; pour over chicken. Cover; cook on high for 3-4 hours.

Remove chicken; pour cooking liquid into saucepan. Return chicken to cooker; cover to keep warm. Skim fat from reserved liquid. Blend cold water slowly into cornstarch; stir into hot liquid. Cook and stir till thickened and bubbly. Serve chicken with gravy over hot cooked rice. Makes 6 servings.

Dost thou think, because thou
        art virtuous, there shall be
        no more cakes and ale?
Yes, by Saint Anne; and ginger
        shall be hot i' the mouth too.

                    Shakespeare,
                    from *Twelfth Night*

Orange Chicken Véronique

3 boneless chicken breasts, skin removed
1 Tbsp. vegetable oil
1 cup orange juice
1 cup dry white wine
2 tsp. sugar
¼ tsp. salt
½ tsp. dried marjoram leaves, rubbed
1 tsp. dried thyme, rubbed
2 Tbsp. cornstarch mixed with
2 Tbsp. water
1 cup halved seedless green grapes
Rice

Place chicken breasts between pieces of wax paper and flatten with a mallet. Cut into small portions. Place oil in 12-inch nonstick skillet. Heat over medium-high heat. Add chicken. Cook for 4 to 6 minutes, or until browned on both sides. Drain excess oil from skillet.

With chicken remaining in skillet, add orange juice, wine, sugar, salt, marjoram and thyme. Cover and reduce heat to low. Let simmer for 15 minutes, or until meat is no longer pink and juices run clear. Remove chicken from skillet and place in serving dish. Cover to keep warm and set aside.

Using whisk, stir cornstarch and water mixture into skillet. Add grapes. Cook for 2 minutes, or until sauce is thickened and translucent, stirring constantly. Spoon over chicken. Makes 6 servings. Serve with rice.

Dried herbs and spices don't last forever. When you open the container, take a whiff. If it is not sending forth the aroma you expected, it should be thrown out and replaced. Make a habit of replacing all the dried herbs you have on your shelf with freshly dried herbs from your garden each summer.

Veal Parmigiana

1 lb. very thin veal steak
1 onion, minced
2 cloves garlic, minced
6 Tbsp. olive oil, divided
19-oz. can tomatoes
1¼ tsp. salt
¼ tsp. pepper
8-oz. can tomato sauce
2 Tbsp. fresh oregano
¼ cup fine dry bread crumbs
1 egg, beaten
½ lb. Mozzarella cheese
1 cup Grated Parmesan cheese

Garlic

Cut veal in serving pieces. Cook onion and garlic in 3 tablespoons olive oil, 5 minutes. Add tomatoes, broken with fork; add salt and pepper. Simmer uncovered 10 minutes. Add tomato sauce and oregano then simmer 20 minutes longer. Mix crumbs and ¼ cup grated Parmesan cheese. Dip veal in egg, then in crumbs. Brown in 3 tablespoons oil in skillet. Put in shallow baking dish and pour about ⅔ of tomato mixture over veal, top with Mozzarella, then rest of tomato mixture. Sprinkle with remaining grated cheese. Bake at 375° for 30 minutes. Makes 4 servings.

Good Tip

Making a *bouquet garni* is as simple as tying fresh herbs together to make a bundle and dropping them into the saucepan.

Ginger Salmon

Ginger Marinade:
2 Tbsp. chopped fresh mint
2 Tbsp. soy sauce
2 Tbsp. fresh lime juice
1 Tbsp. brown sugar, firmly packed
1 tsp. grated lime peel
1 tsp. grated fresh ginger
1 tsp. olive oil
½ tsp. freshly ground pepper
6-8 pieces salmon fillet or steak, skinned

Herbs to Dry
Aniseed
Bay
Caraway seed
Coriander seed
Cumin seed
Dill & seed
Fennel & seed
Hyssop
Lavender
Marigold
Marjoram
Parsley
Rosemary
Sage
Savory
Tarragon
Thyme

Prepare ginger marinade by combining all ingredients in a small bowl. Place salmon in shallow glass dish and spoon on marinade, turning once to coat. (Can be done up to 24 hours ahead. Keep refrigerated.) Preheat broiler. Line jelly-roll pan with foil. Arrange salmon on pan and spoon marinade on top. Broil 4 inches from heat source without turning until fish is opaque throughout, 8 to 10 minutes. Let stand 5 minutes. Serve with Herb Sauce. Makes 6 servings.

Herb Sauce:

½ cup sour cream
2 cups loosely packed cilantro leaves
2 cups loosely packed mint leaves
½ cups loosely packed parsley leaves
2 jalapeño chiles, minced
1 Tbsp. fresh lime juice
¼ tsp. salt
½ tsp. freshly ground pepper

Mint

Combine all ingredients in blender or processor until smooth.

Baked Halibut

4 halibut steaks
1 tsp. salt
Black pepper to taste
3 Tbsp. butter, melted
2 Tbsp. fresh dill, minced
1 cup canned tomatoes
½ tsp. sugar
1 medium onion, thinly sliced
½ cup heavy whipping cream

Preheat oven to 400°. Place halibut in buttered baking dish; sprinkle with salt and pepper. Brush with melted butter. Sprinkle with dill. Crush tomatoes with sugar and spread over fish. Cover with onion. Bake 20 minutes. Pour cream over fish and bake 10 minutes longer. Serve hot. Serves 4.

Herbed Cucumber Sauce

1 medium cucumber
½ cup plain yogurt
  or sour cream
½ cup mayonnaise
2 Tbsp. lemon juice
2 Tbsp. fresh parsley,
  chopped
1 Tbsp. fresh chives,
  chopped
1 Tbsp. fresh dillweed,
  chopped
Pinch ground red pepper

Peel cucumber. Cut in half lengthwise, scoop out seeds, then slice into half-moons. Combine all ingredients in a small bowl, toss to mix and chill until serving time. Garnish with a strip of twisted cucumber peel. Serve with fish dishes. Makes 2 cups.

Broiled Flounder with Pesto

3 Tbsp. butter or margarine, melted
Four 6 oz. flounder fillets
1 Tbsp. lemon juice
1 Tbsp. lemon thyme, minced
¼ cup fresh pesto

Thyme

Line a shallow baking pan with aluminum foil and lightly brush foil with half the butter. Arrange fillets in the pan and brush fish with the remaining butter. Sprinkle fish with lemon juice and spread with pesto. Broil 5 inches from heat for 10 minutes or until fish flakes easily. Makes 4 servings.

Sage Butter

½ cup fresh sage leaves
1 large green onion
½ cup butter, softened
½ tsp. lemon juice
¼ tsp. freshly ground pepper

Blend all ingredients in a processor thoroughly.
Makes ½ cup.

Herbed Lasagna

Oregano

1 box lasagna noodles
1½ lbs. ground chuck
1 large jar spaghetti sauce with mushrooms
1 large carton cottage cheese, small curd
2 eggs, beaten
¼ cup basil
¼ cup oregano
¼ cup Parmesan cheese, grated
24 oz. Mozzarella cheese, shredded

Cook noodles as directed on package. Brown ground chuck; drain; then add spaghetti sauce and simmer for about 15-20 minutes. Mix cottage cheese, eggs, herbs, and Parmesan cheese. Store in refrigerator until ready to use. Grease 9x13-inch pan. Layer noodles, Mozzarella cheese, cottage cheese mixture and meat sauce. Repeat layers. Bake at 350° for 30 minutes. Let cool for 10 minutes. Serves 6.

Easy Marinara Sauce

46-oz. can tomato juice
1 Tbsp. sugar
2 medium green peppers, chopped
1 medium red pepper, chopped
1 small onion, minced
¼ cup fresh basil, chopped
1 Tbsp. fresh oregano, chopped
Dash of garlic powder or to taste

Combine all ingredients in a large saucepan and simmer uncovered for 45 minutes. Serve over cooked spaghetti or noodles. Makes approximately 5 cups.

Parslied Pasta with Pecans

1 cup pecans
1 lb. fettuccine
½ cup olive oil
Salt
Black pepper, freshly ground to taste
½ cup Parmesan cheese, freshly grated
½ cup Italian parsley, minced

Toast pecans in a dry skillet until lightly brown; chop coarsely and set aside. Drop fettuccine into boiling, lightly salted water and cook until al denté. Drain pasta and immediately transfer to a warm bowl. Add oil, salt, and pepper. Toss to coat all strands. Divide pasta among 4 warm plates. Top with pecans, cheese and parsley. Serve at once. Serves 4.

Parsley

Herbal Trees
Broom
Elder
Hawthorn
Juniper
Linden
Norway Spruce
Silver Birch
Walnut

Garlic Fettuccine with Ham

Rosemary

2 cloves garlic, crushed
1 Tbsp. butter or margarine
1½-2 cups thinly sliced ham, cooked and shredded
1 cup green peas
12 oz. fettuccine, cooked and kept hot
½ cup butter or margarine, softened
1 tsp. fresh rosemary, finely minced
1 cup Parmesan cheese, grated
8-oz. carton sour cream
Black pepper, freshly ground

Sauté garlic in 1 tablespoon butter in a large skillet over medium heat. Stir in ham and peas. Sauté another 3 minutes. Remove from heat; cover and keep warm. Place hot, cooked fettuccine in a large bowl. Add ½ cup butter, stirring until melted; add rosemary, cheese and sour cream. Stir gently, until well mixed. Add the ham mixture carefully; add pepper, and serve immediately. Makes 6 servings.

Roasted Garlic & Basil Pesto

1 garlic bulb
1 tsp. olive oil
2 cups fresh basil leaves
2 garlic cloves
¼ cup freshly grated Parmesan cheese
¼ cup pecans
¼ cup margarine, softened
2 Tbsp. olive oil
1 Tbsp. lemon juice

Cut off pointed end of garlic bulb. Spread apart whole cloves, leaving tight outer covering intact. Place garlic on a piece of aluminum foil; drizzle 1 teaspoon of olive oil and fold foil to seal. Bake at 425° for 30 minutes. Cool. Squeeze pulp from roasted garlic cloves into food processor bowl. Add remaining ingredients. Process until smooth. Makes ¾ cup.

Herbed Fettuccine Primivera

1 cup broccoli florets
1 cup sliced zucchini
½ cup diced red or green pepper
½ cup chopped onion
2 Tbsp. fresh basil, chopped
¾ cup butter or margarine
2 medium tomatoes, cut into wedges
½ cup sliced mushrooms
12-oz. pkg. fettuccine noodles, cooked and drained
Parmesan cheese, freshly grated

In a large skillet, over medium heat, cook broccoli, zucchini, pepper, onion and basil in butter until vegetables are tender. Stir in tomatoes and mushrooms. Toss vegetable mixture with hot fettuccine. Serve with Parmesan cheese. Serves 5.

Fresh Pesto with Walnuts

2 cups packed fresh basil
½ cup fresh parsley
¾ cup Parmesan cheese, grated
½ cup walnut pieces
2 large cloves garlic
1 Tbsp. lemon juice or white wine
¼ tsp. salt
¼ tsp. freshly ground black pepper
⅔ cup olive oil

Wash basil leaves thoroughly after removing stems. Drain. In food processor, add basil and the next 7 ingredients. Cover and process until smooth. With processor running, pour oil through food chute in a slow, steady stream until combined. Can freeze for up to 6 months or refrigerate up to 1 week. Makes 1¾ cups.

(Serving suggestion: Toss with hot, cooked pasta and garnish with basil leaves and walnuts.)

Herbed Spaghetti with Scallions

4 cloves garlic, mashed
2 Tbsp. oil
⅓ cup butter or margarine
½ cup scallions, minced
¼ cup dillweed, chopped
¼ cup parsley, minced
Salt and pepper to taste
1 lb. thin spaghetti, cooked and drained

In small saucepan sauté garlic in oil until golden. Discard garlic. Add butter to oil just to melt and stir in scallions and herbs. Heat through. Season with salt and pepper. Pour over hot spaghetti, toss and serve at once. Serves 4.

Oregano Pesto with Toasted Almonds

2 cups fresh parsley leaves
2 cups torn spinach leaves
1 cup fresh oregano leaves
1 Tbsp. lemon juice
2 Tbsp. fresh Parmesan cheese, grated
½ cup sliced almonds, toasted
¼ tsp. salt
3 garlic cloves, peeled
2 Tbsp. olive oil

Combine all ingredients except the oil in a food processor and process until smooth. Slowly add oil through the food chute while the processor remains running. Blend well. Refrigerate until ready to use.

Quiche Lorraine

1 unbaked 9-inch pastry shell
4 slices bacon
¼ cup onion, finely chopped
⅓ cup chives, snipped
1½ cups Swiss cheese, shredded
4 eggs, slightly beaten
1⅓ cups milk
¾ tsp. salt
½ tsp. dry mustard
⅛ tsp. pepper
⅛ tsp. ground nutmeg

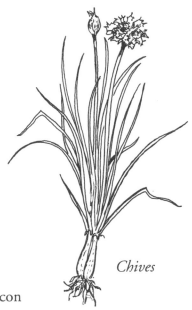

Chives

Preheat oven to 450°. Bake pastry shell for five minutes. Remove from oven. Set oven temperature to 400°. Fry bacon until crisp; drain and crumble. Cook onion until transparent in small amount of bacon fat. Drain. Sprinkle bacon, onion, and chives over bottom of pastry shell. Cover with cheese. Blend together eggs, milk, and seasonings. Pour over cheese. Bake for 10 minutes; reduce heat to 350° and bake 30 to 35 minutes longer or until knife inserted in center comes out clean. Makes 8 servings.

Prepare *Herb Seasoning Packs* consisting of herbs needed for cooking soups, stews, and sauces. Combine sage, thyme, bay, marjoram or oregano, basil (or any desired herbs). Separate into bundle sizes and bind with raffia. String bundles together and snip off as needed and drop into your simmering pot. When food is cooked, remove pack of herbs and discard. These packs will retain their flavor for up to a year.

Grilling

This design is very fitting for equesterians. You reap the benefits of having herbs, yet little time is spent on actual design and gardening, leaving you with time to ride!

Horseshoe Garden

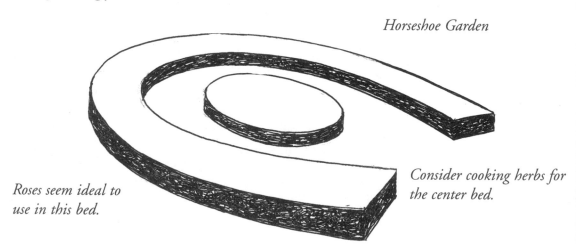

Roses seem ideal to use in this bed.

Consider cooking herbs for the center bed.

Dilled & Grilled Potatoes

8 medium potatoes, scrubbed and dried
6-8 green onions, thinly sliced
1 tsp. fresh dill, chopped
Salt and freshly ground pepper
Butter

Dill

Slice each potato thinly, being careful not to cut completely through. Sprinkle green onions between slices. Season potatoes with dill, salt and pepper. Top each with pieces of butter. Wrap in foil. Prepare grill. Lay foil packages directly on gray coals and cook, turning occasionally, about 1 hour. Serve in foil. Makes 8 servings.

Easy Barbecue Sauce

12-oz. jar orange marmalade
12-oz. bottle chili sauce
¼ cup basil vinegar
1 Tbsp. Worcestershire sauce
1½ tsp. celery seeds

Combine all ingredients in a medium mixing bowl; mix well. Makes about 3 cups.

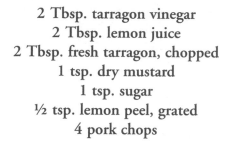

Tarragon Chops on the Grill

2 Tbsp. tarragon vinegar
2 Tbsp. lemon juice
2 Tbsp. fresh tarragon, chopped
1 tsp. dry mustard
1 tsp. sugar
½ tsp. lemon peel, grated
4 pork chops

Tarragon

In a glass baking dish large enough to hold chops in a single layer, combine first 6 ingredients. With a fork prick each chop in several places, then place in the marinade and turn to coat. Cover and refrigerate at least 2 hours or overnight.

Prepare the grill. Grill chops 4-6 inches over medium-hot coals 7-8 minutes per side for medium. Brush occasionally with any remaining marinade.
(To oven broil, broil 6 minutes per side.) Makes 4 servings.

Shake Those Seeds
In order to have uniform distribution of seeds in your garden, use spice bottles which have the shaker holes. They are just right for planting those tiny seeds. Holes will vary, so experiment to find the right size for the seed you are planting.

Grilled Onions with Basil Vinegar Oil

½ cup olive oil
¼ cup basil vinegar
2 Tbsp. fresh basil, chopped
6 red onions, peeled and halved, horizontally

Whisk oil into vinegar very slowly. Add basil, stirring well. Spoon over onions in baking dish. Do not use aluminum. Marinate 2-3 hours at room temperature, turning onions occasionally.

Prepare the grill. Place onions cut side down on grill and cook until brown, about 10 minutes per side, basting frequently. Serves 12.

Simple Sample Pesto

2 cups basil leaves, packed
4 cloves garlic, chopped
2 Tbsp. pine nuts
½ cup olive oil
½ cup freshly grated Parmesan cheese

In a processor, mix all ingredients until smooth. Store tightly sealed in the refrigerator.

Roasted Red Peppers

4 large red bell peppers
Basil leaves

Basil

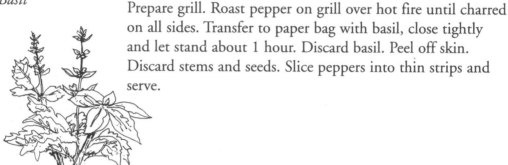

Prepare grill. Roast pepper on grill over hot fire until charred on all sides. Transfer to paper bag with basil, close tightly and let stand about 1 hour. Discard basil. Peel off skin. Discard stems and seeds. Slice peppers into thin strips and serve.

Onion & Tomato Salsa

1 Tbsp. olive oil
1 small onion, chopped
1 clove garlic, chopped
2 large ripe tomatoes, chopped
1 small jalapeño pepper, finely chopped
¼ tsp. salt
¼ tsp. freshly ground black pepper
2 Tbsp. fresh basil, coarsely chopped
3 Tbsp. fresh cilantro leaves, chopped

In a medium saucepan, heat oil over medium heat. Add onion and sauté 5 minutes. Stir in garlic and sauté until soft. Remove from heat. Stir in tomatoes, jalapeño, salt, black pepper, and basil. Cover and refrigerate at least 30 minutes before serving to blend flavors. Stir in cilantro just before serving. Makes about 1 cup.

Quesadillas on the Grill

¼ cup grated jalapeño Monterey Jack cheese
1 Tbsp. diced tomato
1 Tbsp. cilantro, chopped
Fresh salsa
Ripe olives
Flour tortilla

Sprinkle cheese, tomato, cilantro, and fresh salsa and olives
on half a flour tortilla. Fold tortilla over filling and grill until
slightly browned, turning once. Cut into thirds and serve.

Winter Birdfeeders for our Winged Friends

Creating feeders for our feathered friends is a simple and fun activity for the
children on a cold, winter's day or while waiting for Santa!

Pinecones:
Combine peanut butter, birdseed, sunflower seeds, and herb seeds. Use popsi-
cle sticks to fill the spaces on the pinecone. Once full, tie a string or ribbon
around the top section of the pinecone. Spread the remaining seeds, and roll
the pinecones around, picking up more seeds. Hang in a tree where it can be
seen from inside the house. The children will love watching the birds. The
peanut butter and seeds will be gone in no time at all.

Orange Halves:
Remove the orange sections from each half. Tie a string from four points coming together at the top. Fill the halves with popcorn, cranberries, coneflower or
blackeyed susan seeds and hang in a tree. The birds will flock!

Zucchini Stuffed Tomato with Basil & Marjoram

Marjoram

4 tomatoes, hollowed out
2 zucchini, chopped
4 green onions, chopped
1 cup shredded basil
¼ cup marjoram, chopped
Parmesan cheese
Olive oil

Fill hollowed-out tomatoes with a mixture of zucchini, onions, basil, marjoram, and Parmesan cheese. Splash olive oil on top and let stand for 5 minutes. Wrap in foil and grill 15-20 minutes or until tender. Serves 4.

Annual Herbs

Anise
Basil
Borage
Chamomile, German
Chervil
Coriander
Cumin
Dill
Marigold, pot
Marjoram, sweet
Savory, summer

Oven Barbecued Spareribs

3 lbs. spareribs
5.5-oz. can tomato juice from concentrate
½ cup tomato catsup
½ cup water
3 Tbsp. Worcestershire sauce
¼ cup sweet & sour sauce (can substitue ⅓ c. brown sugar)
1 small onion, minced
1 Tbsp. parsley, minced
1 Tbsp. basil, minced
1 small clove garlic, minced
1 Tbsp. basil vinegar

Cut ribs into serving size pieces; place in a 13 x 9-inch baking pan. Bake at 400° for 30 minutes.

Combine remaining ingredients; mix well. Spoon over ribs. Reduce heat to 350° and bake an additional 1½ hours or until tender. Makes 4 servings.

Indoor Herbs

Basil, Dark Opal
Basil, Dwarf Green
Chervil
Chives (Grolau)
Dill Bouquet
Oregano
Parsley
Summer Savory

Grilled Marinated Shrimp

Cilantro

1½ cups pineapple juice
½ cup light rum
¼ cup lime juice
2 Tbsp. chopped fresh cilantro
1 tsp. rosemary, ground
1 tsp. minced garlic
1 tsp. salt
½ tsp. freshly ground black pepper
2 lbs. medium to large shrimp in shells

Combine pineapple juice, rum, lime juice, cilantro, rosemary, garlic, salt and pepper in large bowl. Add shrimp, cover and refrigerate 2-4 hours.

Prepare grill. Thread shrimp on skewers and grill over medium to hot coals until opaque throughout, 1 to 3 minutes per side. Makes 6 servings. Note: Leaving shell on protects the shrimp from burning during grilling.

Cilantro Butter with Lime

½ cup butter, softened
1 tsp. fresh lime juice
1 Tbsp. chopped fresh cilantro

Blend all ingredients and chill.
Makes ½ cup.

Grilled Flank Steak with Cilantro Honey Sauce

½ cup fresh lime juice
¼ cup canola oil
1 jalapeño pepper, finely minced
1 Tbsp. chopped fresh cilantro
2 garlic cloves, minced
1 tsp. chopped fresh sage
2 flank steaks (1½ lbs. each), trimmed
Salt and freshly ground black pepper
Cilantro Honey Sauce

Combine first 6 ingredients in a non-aluminum baking dish. Add steaks, turning to coat. Cover and refrigerate at least 3 hours, turning 1 or 2 times. Remove from refrigerator 30 minutes prior to grilling.

Prepare grill. Grill steak over medium to hot coals 6 to 7 minutes per side. Let stand 5 minutes. Slice very thinly against the grain. Serve with Cilantro Honey Sauce. Makes 8 servings.

Companion Plants

Basil (tomatoes)
Borage (strawberries)
Chives (carrots)
Garlic (roses, carrots)
Horseradish (potatoes)
Nasturtium (beans, squash, cabbage)
Tansy (cucumbers)

Cilantro Honey Sauce

Tarragon

¼ cup honey
¼ cup fresh lime juice
2 Tbsp. canola oil
2 Tbsp. tarragon vinegar
1 Tbsp. prepared mustard
2 garlic cloves, peeled
½ tsp. salt
1 Tbsp. cilantro
1 Tbsp. freshly chopped cilantro

Combine all but 1 tablespoon freshly chopped cilantro in a processor and blend until smooth. Stir in remaining cilantro. Makes about 1 cup.

Evergreen Perennial Herbs

Germander
Horehound
Hyssop
Lavender
Rue
Sage
Salad Burnet
Santolina
Savory, winter
Southernwood
Thyme

Cilantro Chicken

½ cup Worcestershire sauce
¼ cup white wine
2 Tbsp. mustard
½ cup chopped cilantro
6 green onions, thinly sliced
4 broiler-fryer chicken breast and leg quarters

In a small bowl, combine Worcestershire sauce, wine, mustard, cilantro and green onions. Place chicken in one layer in glass baking dish. Pour marinade over chicken, turning in baking dish to coat both sides of each piece with marinade. Cover and refrigerate at least 3 hours.

Prepare grill and oil grid well. Place chicken on grid, skin side down. Grill, covered, 4 to 5 inches over medium-hot coals 20 minutes, turning occasionally and brushing often with marinade left in baking dish. Grill 5 to 10 minutes longer, breast side up, until chicken is fork tender and fully cooked. Makes 4 to 6 servings.

Note: Do not brush cooked chicken with any remaining marinade before serving. Chicken must be cooked about 5 minutes after final brushing with marinade to eliminate any danger of salmonella food poisoning from marinade that has been in contact with raw chicken. Discard any leftover marinade.

Cilantro

When grilling, sprinkle the charcoal with dampened dried herbs such as bay leaves, fennel, marjoram; or use fresh herbs such as rosemary, thyme, dill, or sage. The herbs will give a subtle flavor to your grilled meats and vegetables.

Grilled Tarragon Steak

1 can beer
½ cup chili sauce
¼ cup vegetable oil
2 Tbsp. soy sauce
1 Tbsp. Dijon-style mustard
½ tsp. hot sauce
⅛ tsp. liquid smoke
½ cup coarsely chopped onion
1 Tbsp. chopped tarragon
2 cloves garlic, crushed
3 lb. sirloin steak, 1-2 inches thick

Combine all ingredients except steak. Simmer in a medium saucepan 30 minutes. Brush steak with sauce, and place on grill 4 inches from medium coals; grill 15 minutes on each side or until desired doneness. Baste frequently with sauce. Remove from grill and serve with remaining sauce. Makes 6-8 servings.

Horseradish Cream Sauce

2 Tbsp. prepared horseradish
1 tsp. tarragon vinegar
½ tsp. sugar
½ tsp. dry mustard
¼ cup whipping cream, softly whipped
Salt and freshly ground black pepper

Combine first 4 ingredients in small bowl and blend well. Fold in whipped topping. Taste and season with salt and pepper. Refrigerate until time to serve.

Vegetables

Start a collection of thymes, basils, or lavenders in a ladder garden.

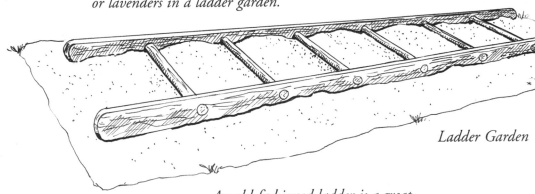

Ladder Garden

An old-fashioned ladder is a great way to create an instant garden. Easy to prepare the garden in the springtime and summer upkeep is a breeze.

Mediterranean Black-eyed Peas

2 Tbsp. olive oil
1 small onion, chopped
1 clove garlic, minced
15-oz. can black-eyed peas, undrained
1 tomato, finely chopped
2 Tbsp. fresh parsley, coarsely chopped
1 Tbsp. fresh oregano

In small saucepan, sauté onions and garlic in olive oil until tender. Add all other ingredients. Cover and cook on low heat until tender.

Wrap herbs in a dampened paper towel and place in a plastic bag. Store in the refrigerator. This will preserve them for about five days. Some herbs are hardier than others, so just check from time to time and discard leaves which are beginning to wilt.

Potatoes in Lemon Butter Sauce

4 medium potatoes, peeled and thickly sliced
Water
6 Tbsp. butter
3 Tbsp. lemon juice
⅓ cup Parmesan cheese
2 slices bacon, cooked and drained
1 Tbsp. parsley, chopped
1 tsp. thyme leaves
1 Tbsp. chives

In medium saucepan, boil potatoes in enough water to cover potatoes. Cook until fork tender. Drain. In small skillet, melt butter and add lemon juice. Add all other ingredients and simmer on low until flavors blend, approximately 5 minutes. Serves 4.

Little Mary's Spanish Casserole

1 large green pepper, chopped
1 large onion, chopped
3 Tbsp. cooking oil
6-oz. pkg. noodles
14.5-oz. can tomatoes
15-oz. can cream style corn
6.5-oz. can mushrooms and liquid
1 tsp. cilantro, finely chopped
1 tsp. basil, chopped
3 tablespoons chili powder
Salt and pepper, to taste
Parmesan cheese, grated

Sauté green pepper and onion in cooking oil. Cook noodles 10 minutes and drain. Mix all ingredients with noodles except Parmesan cheese. Bake at 300° for 20-25 minutes in casserole dish. Add cheese to top, if desired, the last 5 minutes of baking time.

"I have an extensive flower border, in which I am fond of placing handsome plants or fragrant. Those of mere curiosity I do not aim at, having too many other cares to bestow more than a moderate attention to them."

Thomas Jefferson,
letter to Bernard McMahon,
April 8, 1811.

Foiled Again Onions

4 large whole red onions, peeled
3 Tbsp. thyme butter, softened
Salt and pepper
Foil
Thyme Butter

Preheat oven to 375°. Slice off the top ½-inch of the stem end of each onion. Spread thyme butter over the cut surfaces and season with salt and pepper. Place each onion on a large square of foil. Wrap each onion up tightly and put in oven. Bake about 1 hour. Serve while still in foil. Serves 4.

Thyme Butter

½ stick butter, softened
½ tsp. lemon juice
2 Tbsp. thyme, chopped

Combine all ingredients thoroughly. Makes ¼ cup.

Calories in Herbs & Spices

Herb/Spice	Cal./tsp.
Basil leaves	3
Bay leaves	5
Caraway seed	8
Cardamon seed	6
Celery seed	11
Cinnamon	6
Coriander seed	6
Cumin seed	7
Dill seed	9
Fennel seed	8
Garlic powder	5
Ginger	6
Marjoram	4
Nutmeg	11
Oregano	6
Parsley flakes	4
Black pepper	9
White pepper	9
Poppy seed	13
Rosemary leaves	5
Sage	4
Savory	5
Tarragon	5
Thyme	5

Fresh Corn with Chives

Salt
2 qts. water
5 ears of fresh corn
4 Tbsp. fresh chives, finely chopped
Black pepper, freshly ground
2 Tbsp. extra-virgin olive oil

Bring a pot of lightly salted water to a boil. Add the corn, turn off the heat and cover the pot. Let the corn stand in the water 3 minutes. Remove from the water. Cut off the kernels. Toss with the chives and pepper. Drizzle with the olive oil. Serve warm. Makes 4 servings.

Herbed Corn in Tomato Cups

1 onion, chopped
3 Tbsp. butter or margarine
2 cups whole-kernel corn
½ tsp. salt
Pepper, freshly ground
¼ cup minced fresh herbs (parsley, thyme, basil, or savory)
4 large tomatoes

Savory

Sauté onion in butter until lightly browned; add corn, salt, pepper and herbs. Slice top off each tomato and scoop out centers. Fill tomatoes with corn mixture. Place tomatoes into a shallow baking dish and bake in a 375° oven for 30 minutes. Makes 4 servings.

California Succotash with Dill & Savory

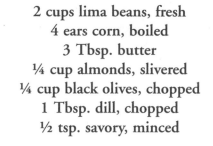

2 cups lima beans, fresh
4 ears corn, boiled
3 Tbsp. butter
¼ cup almonds, slivered
¼ cup black olives, chopped
1 Tbsp. dill, chopped
½ tsp. savory, minced

Dill

Cook lima beans in small amount of boiling water 10 minutes; add corn, cut from ears. Cook 10 minutes longer. Melt 3 tablespoons butter, add almonds and brown lightly. Add browned almonds, olives, dill, and savory to drained succotash. Makes 4 servings.

Limas in Sour Cream

2 pkg. frozen lima beans
2 Tbsp. green onion, chopped
2 Tbsp. diced pimento, drained
2 Tbsp. butter, melted
1 cup sour cream
2 tsp. thyme, minced

Cook beans according to package directions; drain and set aside. Sauté onion and pimento in butter until onion is tender; remove from heat and add sour cream and thyme, stirring well. Add sour cream mixture to lima beans; stir until blended. Cook over low heat until thoroughly heated. Serve immediately. Makes 6 servings.

Rice & Pine Nut Pilaf

2 tsp. olive oil
1½ cups chopped onion
4 garlic cloves, minced
5 cups hot cooked rice
⅓ cup fresh basil, chopped
⅓ cup pine nuts, toasted
½ tsp. salt
¼ tsp. pepper
Basil sprig, for garnish

Heat olive oil in a large nonstick skillet over medium heat. Add onion and garlic, and sauté 3 minutes or until tender. Combine onion mixture, rice, and remaining ingredients in a bowl; toss well. Garnish with a basil sprig. Makes 6 servings.

> To throw a perfume on the violet is wasteful and ridiculous excess.
>
> Shakespeare, from *King John*

Green Beans Almondine

1 lb. green beans, washed and broken
½ cup water
1 clove garlic, minced
1 Tbsp. butter
1 Tbsp. Worcestershire sauce
1 tsp. salt
Freshly ground black pepper
¼ cup sliced almonds

> When substituting dried herbs for fresh, use a third of the amount of fresh herb called for.

Cook green beans 15-20 minutes. Drain. Add water, garlic, butter, Worcestershire sauce, salt and pepper. Cook 15 minutes longer. Stir in sliced almonds.

Greek Onions with Olive Oil & Crusty Bread

1 lb. small white sweet onions
½ cup tarragon vinegar
1 Tbsp. sugar
1 tsp. salt
½ cup extra-virgin olive oil
Fresh oregano, minced
Italian bread

Oregano

Peel onions, leaving whole. Place in a large pan with enough water to cover onions. Cook over medium heat for 15 minutes. Add water as necessary to keep onions covered. Add vinegar, sugar, and salt. Lower heat and simmer for 1 hour more. Refrigerate until ready to use. Serve cold by placing in small plate and drizzling olive oil and sprinkling with minced oregano. Serve with thick, crusty bread slices. Serves 4.

All gardeners know better than other gardeners.
Chinese Proverb

Baked Tomatoes with Garlic & Basil

1 cup coarse fresh bread crumbs
3 Tbsp. Parmesan cheese, grated
2 Tbsp. olive oil, divided
2 cloves garlic, minced
⅓ cup basil, chopped
5 medium tomatoes

Heat oven to 450°. Mix bread crumbs, Parmesan cheese, 1 tablespoon olive oil, garlic and basil in a medium bowl. Slice about ⅓ off tops of tomatoes and cut across tomatoes partway down twice. Spread tomato open slightly. Place cut sides up in a shallow baking dish. Sprinkle tomatoes with crumb mixture and drizzle with remaining olive oil. Bake 8 to 10 minutes until crumbs are toasted. Serves 5.

To-Die-For Roasted Garlic

Garlic heads (any number)
2 tsp. olive oil per garlic head

Garlic

Remove the outer layer of skin from garlic heads. Cut ½ inch off each head straight across top and place in a shallow baking pan. Drizzle 2 teaspoons olive oil over each head, letting it run between the exposed cloves. Cover with foil and bake 30 minutes in a 350° oven. Remove foil and bake 30 to 45 minutes longer or until garlic is tender when pierced with a toothpick. Cool slightly. To serve, peel off cloves and squeeze the roasted garlic onto vegetables or toasted bread.

Quick Herbed Tomato Casserole

28-oz. can whole tomatoes, juice drained and reserved
1½ cups herb-flavored stuffing mix, divided
1 small onion, chopped
1½ tsp. sugar
1 tsp. salt
¼ cup fresh oregano, chopped
1 Tbsp. fresh rosemary, chopped
2 Tbsp. margarine, melted

Cut tomatoes into bite-sized pieces, reserving juice. Combine tomatoes with all other ingredients reserving ½ cup stuffing mix. Mix well. Pour into a greased 1-quart casserole. Combine melted margarine and remaining stuffing mix. Spread over top of casserole and bake at 375° for 45 minutes. Serves 4.

Rosemary

Fried Potatoes with Onions & Parsley

1 small onion, chopped
½ cup vegetable oil
3 large potatoes, peeled and cut into thin strips
¼ cup fresh parsley, chopped
1 Tbsp. fresh oregano
½ tsp. salt
Freshly ground black pepper

In a large frying pan, sauté onion in oil until transparent.
Add potatoes. Cover and cook over medium heat 10 minutes
or until tender. Turn over potatoes and cook, uncovered 5
minutes. Combine remaining ingredients and sprinkle over
potatoes. Cook potatoes, uncovered 5 more minutes, turning
occasionally to brown all sides. Remove potatoes to serving
dish. Makes 4 servings.

Crush dried herbs gently with a mortar and pestle to
enhance their flavor. Slightly bruising fresh plants will
also increase their effectiveness.

Spanish Rice with Garlic & Oregano

2 Tbsp. olive oil
1 onion, chopped
1 green bell pepper, chopped
2½ cups tomatoes, mashed
2 cloves garlic, minced
1 tsp. dried or 1 Tbsp. fresh oregano
1 tsp. salt
½ tsp. sugar
2 cups cooked rice
¼ lb. grated sharp or mild Cheddar cheese

Heat oil over medium heat in frying pan adding onion and pepper. Cook until brown, stirring constantly. Add tomatoes, garlic, oregano, salt, and sugar. Simmer 5 minutes and add cooked rice. Turn into greased baking dish and top with cheese. Cover and bake 20 minutes at 350°. Uncover and increase heat to 400° and cook until beginning to brown. Serves 6-8.

Our gardens nourish my soul inspiring the most intimate details and observations on infinity... they are medicinal nourishment for my body — a tranquil setting for natural healing.

Jim Asher

Green Beans Provençal

4 cups fresh green beans
1 tsp. olive oil
½ cup sliced green onions
4 garlic cloves, crushed
2 cups tomatoes, seeded and thinly sliced
2 Tbsp. fresh basil, chopped
¼ tsp. salt
¼ tsp. pepper
Parmesan cheese, grated

Steam green beans, covered, 5 minutes or until tender. Drain well, and set aside. Heat oil in a large skillet over medium heat. Add onions and garlic; sauté 1 minute. Add green beans; sauté 3 to 4 minutes. Add tomato and remaining ingredients. Cook 2 minutes longer and pour into a serving bowl. Sprinkle with cheese and serve. Makes 4 servings.

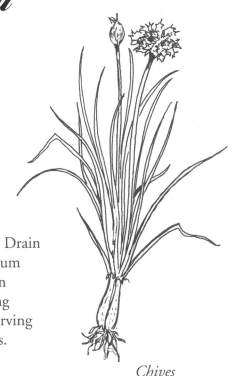

Chives

Peppermint tea is said to stimulate that part of the brain that figures math.

Garlic Mashed Potatoes

3 lbs. potatoes, peeled and cubed
4 whole cloves garlic
Water
¾ cup milk
½ cup margarine
Salt and pepper
Parsley

In large saucepan, combine potatoes and garlic. Add water to cover and heat to a boil. Reduce heat and simmer until potatoes are tender. Remove from heat; drain. Place potatoes and garlic in large bowl. In saucepan, over low heat, heat milk and margarine until margarine melts. Whip potatoes, gradually adding milk mixture until smooth. Season to taste and garnish with parsley.

Rosemary Potato Wedges

5 red potatoes
1 Tbsp. olive oil
1 tsp. dried rosemary
¼ tsp. salt
¼ tsp. pepper

Preheat oven to 450°. Cut each potato lengthwise into 6 wedges. Pat dry with paper towels; place in an 11x7-inch baking dish. Drizzle with oil. Sprinkle with rosemary and remaining ingredients; toss well. Bake for 30 minutes or until tender, stirring occasionally. Makes 6 servings.

Ginger Spinach with Garlic

3 lbs. fresh spinach, each leaf well washed
1 tsp. fresh ginger, grated
1 clove garlic, finely minced
1 jalapeño pepper, finely minced
Salt to taste
½ cup fresh cilantro, finely chopped
3-4 Tbsp. olive oil
¼ cup sliced almonds

Ginger

Bring 4 quarts salted water to boil and place spinach into water. When it comes to a boil again, cook spinach 2 to 3 minutes. Drain and rinse under cold water. In a vegetable spinner, remove as much water as possible.

In a food processor, combine spinach, ginger, garlic, jalapeño pepper, salt, cilantro, and 2 tablespoons olive oil and blend to a smooth paste. Pour spinach mixture into an oven-proof casserole dish. In a small skillet, sauté nuts in remaining olive oil just until they begin to change color. Stir nuts into the spinach and bake in a preheated 350° oven until heated through.

Add some style to your next barbecue. Make flavor sticks with herb branches, lemon grass, and even spice sticks.

Sweets

Containers are ideal for gardeners who are unable to incorporate gardens into their landscape. With containers, herbs are at your fingertips to enjoy aromas and cuisines in as big a way as you like.

Container Gardening

Placed near an outdoor seating area, these herbs will scent the air all summer.

Minted Fruit Ambrosia

1 banana, peeled and sliced
2 peaches, peeled and sliced
1 kiwi, peeled and sliced
20-oz. can pineapple chunks, undrained
½ cup coconut
½ cup grapes, red seedless
½ cup grapes, green seedless
½ cup sugar
1 Tbsp. fresh mint, finely chopped
11-oz. can Mandarin oranges, undrained
¼ tsp. almond extract

Mix all and let sit 1 hour before serving. Serves 6.*

*Serve over thinly sliced shortcake with whipped topping and garnish with mint.

Shortcake:

1 cup all-purpose flour
1½ tsp. baking powder
½ tsp. salt
¼ cup margarine, melted
¾ cup sugar
1 tsp. aniseed
½ cup milk
1 egg

Mix until well blended. Pour into buttered loaf pan. Cook in a 350° preheated oven for 20 minutes or until firm.

Anise

Lemon Thyme Crisps

2 cups self-rising flour
½ tsp. baking soda
¾ cup butter, softened
¾ cup sugar
1 egg
1 Tbsp. grated lemon peel
1 Tbsp. lemon juice
⅓ cup fresh lemon thyme, finely chopped
⅓ cup chopped pecans
3 Tbsp. sugar

Stir together the flour and baking soda; set aside. In a large bowl, whip the butter and ¾ cup sugar until light and fluffy; add the egg and mix well. Add lemon peel, lemon juice, and lemon thyme. Stir in the dry ingredients until thoroughly combined. Wrap and chill the dough for at least 1 hour.

Shape the dough into 1-inch balls. Combine nuts with the 3 tablespoons sugar. Roll balls of dough in sugar and nut mixture until coated. Place the balls 2 inches apart on an ungreased baking sheet. Flatten cookies slightly with a fork. Bake in a 350° oven for 10-12 minutes or until edges are golden. Cool. Makes about 5 dozen cookies.

Vanilla beans are the pods of an orchid found in Central and South America. To cure, the pods are first blanched, then sun-dried by day and covered with blankets to sweat each night for several months. The beans shrink about 400 percent and gradually darken.

Apple Molasses Muffins with Rosemary & Thyme

4 cups all-purpose flour
¾ cup molasses
¾ cup packed brown sugar
½ cup butter or margarine, softened
⅓ cup milk
2 tsp. baking soda
2 tsp. ground cinnamon
1 tsp. ground allspice
1 tsp. rosemary, minced
1 tsp. thyme, minced
1 tsp. salt
2 eggs
3 large red cooking apples, peeled and diced
¾ cup walnuts, chopped

Rosemary & Thyme

Preheat oven to 375°. Grease and flour eighteen 3-inch muffin pan cups. Into large bowl, measure all ingredients except apples and walnuts. With processor at low speed, process until blended. Stir in apples and walnuts. Spoon batter into muffin pan cups to come almost to the top of each cup. Bake 25 minutes or until toothpick inserted in center of muffin comes out clean. Cool muffins in pans on wire racks 10 minutes. Remove from pans. Serve warm. Makes 18 muffins.

Lemon Thyme & Fennel Pound Cake

Fennel

½ cup butter, softened
1½ cups sugar
Pinch of salt
5 large eggs
2 cups all-purpose flour
2 Tbsp. fennel seed, toasted and crushed
1 Tbsp. lemon thyme, minced
½ Tbsp. grated lemon zest
1 tsp. vanilla extract
2 Tbsp. fresh lemon juice

In a large bowl cream butter, sugar and salt together. Add eggs, one at a time, beating well after each addition. Stir in flour, fennel seed, lemon thyme, and zest. Add vanilla and lemon juice and blend well. Pour batter into 3 greased, floured and waxed paper-lined 5¾x3x2⅛-inch loaf pans and bake in preheated 325° oven 30-40 minutes or until tester comes out clean. Cool 10 minutes.

Glaze:

⅓ cup lemon juice
½ cup sugar
3 Tbsp. candied julienned lemon zest

In a small saucepan over low heat combine lemon juice, sugar and zest and stir until sugar dissolves.

Pierce loaves all over with a skewer and spoon glaze over loaves. Cool in pan. To remove from pan, run a sharp knife around the edges of the cake to loosen from the sides. Garnish with lemon peel curls. May wrap and refrigerate up to 1 week or freeze up to 1 month.

Violet Jam

1 pkg. powdered pectin
2½ cups water
½ cup lemon juice
3 cups sugar
1 cup violet blossoms, tightly packed
⅓ cup lemon rind, shredded into slivers

Combine the pectin, water, and lemon juice. Bring to a boil;
add the sugar; stir, and boil for 3 minutes. Gently stir in the
violets and lemon rind slivers. Remove from heat immediat-
ley. Pour into hot sterilized jars and seal. Process 5 minutes
in boiling water.

Herb Honey

Use: (your choice)
Anise
Coriander
Fennel
Lavender
Marjoram
Mint
Rosemary
Sage
Scented Geranium
Thyme

Bruise fresh herb leaves or seeds slightly and put into medium saucepan. Add
amount of honey you wish to flavor. Cook over low heat until just warm,
about 2 minutes. (High heat will destroy honey). Pour into sterilized jars and
seal. Store at room temperature.

Squash Bread

18-oz. box yellow cake mix
3.9-oz. box vanilla instant pudding mix
4 eggs
¼ cup vegetable oil
3 cups squash, peeled and grated
¼ cup fresh basil, finely chopped
½ tsp. salt
1 tsp. cinnamon
1 cup chopped nuts

Combine all ingredients and pour into 2 greased and floured loaf pans. Bake in a preheated 350° oven for 50 minutes or until knife comes out clean. Makes 2 loaves.

It is a golden maxim to cultivate the garden for the nose, and the eyes will take care of themselves.

Robert Louis Stevenson

Lemon Herb Tea Bread

¾ cup milk
1 Tbsp. chopped lemon balm
1 Tbsp. chopped lemon thyme
2 cups self-rising flour
6 Tbsp. butter, softened
1 cup sugar
2 eggs
1 Tbsp. zest of lemon

Lemon Glaze:

3 Tbsp. lemon juice
Powdered sugar

Lemon Balm

Preheat oven to 325°. Butter and flour loaf pan. Heat milk, but not to a boil. Add herbs and let sit until cooled. Measure flour and put into bowl. In another larger bowl, cream butter, gradually adding sugar. Add eggs and lemon zest. Add flour alternately with herb milk and mix well. Pour batter into loaf pan and bake for 50 minutes or until sides pull away from pan. Remove from pan and place loaf on platter.

Make glaze by combining lemon juice and sugar until thick but pourable. Drizzle over bread while still warm. Garnish with sprigs of lemon thyme. Makes 1 loaf.

Seasonings

Vinaigrettes
Vinegars
Oils
Rubs
Seasoning Mixes
Marinades

Herbal Vinaigrettes

Vinaigrettes are sauces made using vinegars, oil, and herbs. They add their own distinctive flavors and instill a tantalizing taste to the dishes they accompany. They are very easy to prepare and can be mixed ahead of time. These can be used on salads, meats, or vegetables.

Lemon Thyme Vinaigrette

1 tsp. Dijon mustard
¼ cup fresh lemon juice
½ tsp. kosher salt
¼ tsp. freshly ground pepper
½ cup extra-virgin olive oil
¼ cup lemon thyme, chopped

Whisk mustard, lemon juice, salt, and pepper together. Whisking constantly, slowly drizzle in the olive oil. Add thyme. Makes about ¾ cup.

In the Victorian language of flowers, violets represent humility and modesty.

Basil & Tomato Vinaigrette

¼ cup red onion, diced
3 Tbsp. red wine vinegar
¼ cup thyme, finely chopped
½ tsp. black pepper, freshly ground
⅓ cup olive oil
1 medium tomato, very ripe, peeled and seeded, then diced
⅓ cup fresh basil, chopped

In a medium bowl combine onion, vinegar, thyme, and pepper. Let stand for 15 minutes. Whisk in olive oil. Add tomato and basil. Refrigerate for at least 1 hour before serving. Let come to room temperature and stir well before using. Makes 1 cup.

Cucumber Vinaigrette

4 cucumbers, peeled, seeded and chopped
¼ cup tarragon vinegar
1 cup virgin olive oil
½ cup chives, chopped

In blender or processor, combine cucumbers, vinegar, and oil. Blend well. Pour into bowl and whisk in chives.

Walnut Vinaigrette

¼ cup tarragon vinegar
1 tsp. Dijon mustard
Salt and freshly ground pepper
½ cup safflower oil (vegetable oil can be substituted)
¼ cup walnut oil
½ cup chopped walnuts (can be toasted for extra flavor)
Basil, chopped

Combine vinegar, mustard, salt and pepper in blender or processor. Slowly pour in both oils through feed chute. Stir in walnuts and drizzle over salad. Sprinkle with basil. Makes 1 cup.

Honey Mustard Vinaigrette

½ cup salad oil
½ cup tarragon vinegar
1 Tbsp. honey
¼ tsp. dry mustard

In a jar with tight-fitting lid, combine all ingredients and shake well. Makes about 1 cup.

Tarragon

Herbal Vinegars

When making vinegar, choose a vinegar that is not stronger in flavor than the herb you are using. Always use a mild flavored vinegar such as white wine vinegar, a distilled or a cider vinegar.

A good rule of thumb: use 1 cup of fresh herbs to 2 cups of vinegar.

Some choices for herbs would include basil, chives, coriander, dill, fennel, garlic, oregano, rosemary, salad burnet, tarragon, and thyme.

Pack a jar or bottle with washed and dried herb leaves. Bruise or crush the leaves slightly to release the flavor. Pour the vinegar over the herb and seal the container with a non-metallic lid. (Note: if you have to use a metal lid, first cover the mouth of the jar with plastic wrap, then place the lid on the jar.) Place in a warm spot, away from direct sunlight, for 2 to 4 weeks, shaking periodically. Do a taste test to see if it has reached the desired strength. Then using a coffee filter, strain into a clean bottle and add a sprig of the herb for identification. Seal tightly and store on your pantry shelf until needed. To restore flavor, simply add fresh herbs.

Use vinegar to flavor salad dressings, vinaigrettes, mayonnaise. Use anywhere you would use vinegar. It is very tasty served with spinach and salads.

Gingered Vinegar

1 cup cider vinegar
5 one-inch pieces dried gingerroot
2 Tbsp. sugar
½ tsp. lemon juice

Combine all ingredients. Let sit for 1 week. Strain and store in a tightly covered bottle.

Basil Vinegar

1 quart jar, wide-mouth
Basil, bruised
Vinegar

Fill jar with bruised basil to about ¾ full. Add vinegar to cover. Cover jar tightly. Do not use a metal lid. Place in a warm, dark place for 2-4 weeks, shaking periodically. After vinegar has reached the desired flavor, strain into a decorative bottle, adding fresh basil to denote the flavor.

Basil

Tarragon Vinegar

Tarragon, 1 good size bunch
White wine vinegar

Lay tarragon leaves out thinly on a rack or on a paper towel for three or four days to lose much of their moisture content. Pack the leaves into a wide-mouthed jar. Cover them completely with the vinegar. Close and let stand for 2-3 weeks. Pour off a little to test for aroma. If it is not strong enough, let stand a while longer. After it reaches the desired strength, strain into a decorative jar adding an identifying sprig of tarragon; or simply leave in the jar with the herbs.

Nasturtium Vinegar

Nasturtium flowers, lightly bruised
White distilled vinegar

Fill a small jar with bruised nasturtium flowers. Cover with vinegar. Seal tightly with non-metallic lid and store on pantry shelf for 2 weeks or until the vinegar reaches a rich color, shaking periodically. Use in salads with mild flavored greens.

Nasturtium

Citrus & Thyme Vinegar

Raspberries (or cranberries)
Kiwi, peeled
Orange
Orange Thyme
Lemon Thyme
White wine vinegar

Place raspberries in the bottom of jar. Slice the kiwi across and place in jar. Peel the orange making long spirals of the peeling. Quarter or section the peeled orange and put into jar. Add the spirals to the jar. Wash and dry bunches of the orange thyme and lemon thyme. Gently bruise the herbs and place into the jar and add enough vinegar to cover all ingredients. Seal with a cork or non-metallic lid. Let stand for at least 2 weeks before using. Strain into a fresh jar and add identifying ingredients or strain as it is used. Good in meat marinades or for fruit salad dressings.

Peppered Vinegar

Peppercorns
1 green onion
Green chiles
Red chiles
1 cup basil, slightly bruised
½ cup savory, slightly bruised
Nasturtium flowers
White wine vinegar

Place peppercorns into bottom of jar. Cut top and bottom of onion and place in jar. Add remaining ingredients using enough vinegar to cover. Seal tightly with a cork or non-metallic lid. Let stand for 2 weeks to mature. Shake the jar periodically to blend flavors. Good for a spicy marinade or salad dressing.

Oils

Oils are great to have already prepared when we need them for cooking. Flavoring oil is simple. Pick, wash, and dry leaves from the herb of your choice and place into a clean bottle with a cork for sealing (or non-metallic lid). Gently bruise the herb before placing into the jar. Cover with extra-virgin olive oil and seal. Shake to mix the freshly released flavor of the herb and the oil. If you use garlic in the oil, keep refrigerated to prevent any chance of botulism.

If there is no garlic in the oil, leave in a warm place about 2 weeks to allow the herbs to infuse the oil with their flavor. After 2 weeks, test for flavor. If it is satisfactory, strain, store in a bottle and place a new sprig of the herb in the bottle for identification. Life of oil is about two or three months before it begins to lose its herbal flavor. You can restore flavor by adding fresh herbs to the oil.

Parsley & Oregano Herb Oil

½ cup parsley
¼ cup oregano
2 cups olive oil

Combine all ingredients in a blender or processor and puree for about 15 seconds. Strain through cheesecloth and store in a tightly covered jar in the refrigerator for up to 1 week. Let the oil come to room temperature before using.

Rosemary Oil

½ cup extra virgin olive oil
¼ cup fresh rosemary (no stems)

Herbs for Bonsai

Curry Plant
Hyssop
Lavender, Dwarf
Rosemary
Rue
Santolina
Sweet Bay

Combine oil and rosemary in a small pan. Heat the oil over moderate heat until bubbles begin to form. Reduce to low and simmer 2-3 minutes longer or until the rosemary has faded and is beginning to crisp. Remove from heat and cool. Strain into a clean jar. Keep refrigerated. Makes ½ cup.

Sage & Garlic Oil

3 garlic cloves, thinly sliced
½ cup extra virgin olive oil
¼ cup whole fresh sage leaves
1 tsp. thyme, chopped

In a small pan, combine the garlic and olive oil. Cook the garlic until golden. Remove garlic to a bowl and add sage leaves and thyme to oil. Cook until leaves are crisp. Add reserved garlic and let cool. Store in refrigerator for up to 1 month. Makes ½ cup.

Sage

Note: Store any oil that is flavored with garlic in the refrigerator to preven botulism.

Smashed Garlic Oil

2 cups virgin olive oil
3 Tbsp. fresh oregano, chopped
3 Tbsp. fresh dill, chopped
½ cup fresh parsley, chopped
4 Tbsp. fresh chives, chopped
6-7 garlic cloves, peeled and smashed

Mix all ingredients in a bowl. Keeps for 1 month refrigerated. Makes 2 cups.

Note: Store any oil that is flavored with garlic in the refrigerator to preven botulism.

Rubs & Seasonings

If you want maximum flavor with minimum effort and investment of time, you must try "dry rubs." These are especially fine for grilling. A concoction of spices and herbs are simply rubbed over the meat prior to placing on the grill or in the oven. Applying "dry rubs" creates a crunchy crust which is extremely flavorful. The spices will brown on the grill, so cook over a medium heat to prevent blackening and scorching of the herbs and spices.

To make a dry rub, mix the spices and herbs together thoroughly. Coat the meat all over by filling your hand and patting on firmly or placing the rub mixture and the food in a plastic bag and shaking.

Keep meat covered and refrigerated until ready to use. You can store the meat with rub already applied in the refrigerator up to 5 hours ahead of cooking time. Keep dry rubs covered and refrigerated to maintain flavors.

Spicy Rub

½ cup ground mustard
½ cup dried oregano leaves
¼ cup crushed red pepper
1 Tbsp. chili powder
2 Tbsp. garlic powder
2 Tbsp. black ground pepper
1 tsp. ground nutmeg
2 tsp. salt

Makes approximately 1¼ cup.

BBQ Rub

2 cups mesquite grill seasoning
½ cup dehydrated minced garlic
½ cup mustard seed
2 tsp. dried thyme
½ cup black cracked pepper
2 Tbsp. rosemary, minced

Makes approximately 2½ cups.

Sage & Lemon Pepper Rub

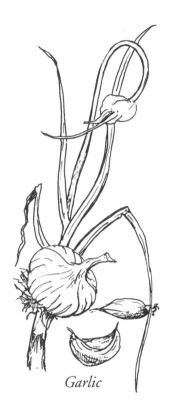

Garlic

¾ cup dried basil leaves
½ cup lemon pepper
½ cup onion powder
½ cup rubbed sage

Makes approximately ½ cup.

Mediterranean Rub

⅓ cup fennel seeds, crushed
2 Tbsp. chives
1 Tbsp. mustard seeds, crushed
1 tsp. lemon pepper
½ tsp. garlic powder
¼ tsp. salt

Makes approximately ½ cup.

Lemon Pepper Rub

1 Tbsp. lemon pepper seasoning
1 Tbsp. onion powder
1 Tbsp. paprika
2 tsp. coarsely ground black pepper
2 tsp. celery seed
1 tsp. coriander seed
2 tsp. garlic powder
1 tsp. salt
1 tsp. dry mustard
1 tsp. ground ginger
½ tsp. ground allspice

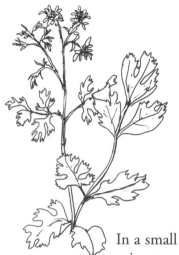

Coriander

In a small bowl combine all ingredients. About 30 minutes prior to grilling, rub mixture over meat. This will spice several pounds of meat. Keep unused portion stored in a tightly closed jar in a cool place.

Rib Rub

2 Tbsp. thyme, minced
1 Tbsp. salt
3 Tbsp. sugar
1 Tbsp. celery seed
1 Tbsp. black pepper
2 Tbsp. paprika

Combine all ingredients in a bowl. Prior to cooking ribs, press dry seasoning by handfuls onto meat.

Bouquet Garni 2

A mixture of aromatic herbs tied up into bundles or into small bags is known as "bouquet garni." Place in a bag (can be a coffee filter, muslin, cheese cloth):

> 1 bay leaf, broken
> 2 sprigs of parsley
> 2 sprigs of thyme
> 2 sprigs of marjoram

Other herbs can be substituted or added such as rosemary, garlic, basil, chervil, chives, savory. Add to casseroles or soups at the beginning of cooking time. Always remove when cooking is complete.

Marjoram

Fish & Seafood Seasoning

> ¼ c. dried parsley
> 3 Tbsp. lemon-pepper seasoning
> 3 Tbsp. dillweed
> 4 Bay leaves, crumbled

Poultry Seasoning

> 1 Tbsp. rubbed sage
> 1 Tbsp. onion powder
> 1 Tbsp. black pepper
> 1 Tbsp. celery seeds
> 1 Tbsp. thyme
> 1 Tbsp. marjoram
> 2 tsp. rosemary
> 2 tsp. garlic powder

Marinades

A marinade is a seasoned liquid used to tenderize and flavor foods. Simply combine your marinade and food in a plastic bag and chill. When grilling, baste foods with the remaining marinade. When making a sauce from leftover marinade, bring it to a boil to kill all bacteria, then continue with the sauce.

Lemon Herb Marinade

Mint

2 tsp. grated lemon zest
⅔ cup fresh lemon juice
¼ cup fresh basil, chopped
¼ cup fresh mint, chopped
¼ cup tarragon vinegar
2 Tbsp. fresh oregano, chopped
1½ Tbsp. olive oil
2 cloves garlic, crushed

Combine all ingredients and stir marinade well. Makes approximately 1¼ cups.

Garlic Steak Marinade

1 cup red wine
½ cup oil
1 clove garlic, crushed
1 bay leaf
1 tsp. oregano

Combine, pour over steak and let stand 4-6 hours.

HERB GARDENING

What is an herb? I have been asked this many times and my answer is never the same. With so many types of plants, it is hard to make one declaration as to what is an herb. An herb is a plant that is considered useful. In my opinion herbs are much more than "useful."

Herbs are an important part of medicine. They have been considered important for treating ailments since pre-history. Today, herbs provide essential elements that make up much of our modern medicine.

Herbs give us personal pleasures with their wonderful, colorful surprises, in their aromas, textures and the promise of something new each day. We grow and gather herbs to season our food and for their beautiful flowers. Herbs may be used to dye cloth or mixed to create the pleasing aroma of potpourri. We place pleasantly scented herbs in our linen cabinets in the form of sachets. We even add herbs to our bath to relax or envigorate our psyche.

Herb growers may garden because they enjoy the feel of the earth, while some growers are crafters growing herbs for the many crafts they enjoy all year long. Some herb growers may grow herbs for the flavor they provide as food seasonings. People grow herbs for all these reasons and use them creatively every day.

For whatever reason you grow herbs, they will certainly provide many hours of pleasure for you whether used in cooking, for crafting, making potpourri, or just walking through the garden.

PLANTING & PROPAGATION OF HERBS

PREPARATION OF GARDEN SOIL

Drainage is one of the most important features of soil preparation for herbs. There are very few herbs that prefer "their feet" sit in wet soil.

Most herbs originated in arid Mediterranean areas, which are known to have poor, rocky soil. Although herbs do tolerate poor conditions in the soil, they have little tolerance and will not produce very pleasing plants and, in turn, certainly not flavorful plants. If the soil is too wet, some herb roots will simply rot away. A compromise must be found.

Thus good drainage is necessary, but some moisture retention is also necessary to provide water for the plant and keep it fed. If the soil is composed of mostly clay, add some sand and organic matter to promote good drainage. If the soil is very light and sandy, add organic matter to help retain water. The "perfect" soil is described as loam which is just the right combination of sand, clay, and organic matter. Loam keeps the moisture in while still draining well.

When we add organic matter it continually decomposes and must be replaced. Prior to planting your garden in the spring, add about 4 inches of organic matter to the soil, such as compost, peat moss, decomposed sawdust, or manure. Work it in well and then top with a thin layer of lime. By planting time the soil will be ready.

PROPAGATION OF HERBS

Increasing the quantity of your favorite plants gives you the freedom to be extravagant when using them in cooking and sharing with your friends. There are several methods to increase the herbs in your garden.

SEEDS

Sowing seed is by far the easiest method of propagating plants. They are easy to gather at the end of the season and sow the next spring or you can purchase packets of seed from most garden centers. Annuals lend themselves best to this method. Dill, anise, and coriander are true annuals and can only be grown from seed. Basil is also very easily grown from seed.

To get an early start, plant seeds indoors or in a cold frame under cover in early spring. Fill a tray with a good, sterile starting medium. Tap the tray and fill with more medium if necessary. Tap the seeds gently onto the soil. Be sure to label the seeds that are being planted. Cover with a light covering of more medium. Set the seed trays in a solid tray with lukewarm water.

When the seedlings reach about 1 inch, transplant them to a pot of their own, placing two or three in each pot. When the plants are well rooted and have their first set of true leaves, clip off all but the strongest plant in each pot.

When plants are well developed, harden them off by exposing them to outside temperatures for short periods each day. Gradually extend the length of time they are exposed to the outdoors each day. They can now be transplanted into the garden after all danger of frosts.

Seeds can be sown directly in the garden also. Dill can be sown as early as 2 weeks before the date of the last expected frost. Basil, anise, and coriander should be sown after all danger of frost.

CUTTINGS

One of the best methods of propagating many plants consists of taking cuttings. Most shrubby type plants do well with this method, such as rosemary.

Stem cuttings are taken by cutting with a razor blade or very sharp knife (scissors will crush the stem) in an angle giving as much surface as possible to come into contact with the soil. Dip the cut stem into a rooting powder and plant in a pot with light soil containing perlite or vermiculite. These ingredients will retain much needed moisture. Water well and allow the excess water to drain out. Cover the pot with plastic and place in sunlight. Keep the soil moist but do not let the pot sit in water. After two weeks, gently tug on the stem. If it pulls easily, it has not taken root. If some resistance is present, the rooting has begun. When fully rooted the plant can be transplanted into the garden.

Root cuttings, especially horseradish, can be easily made by taking the dug-up root and cutting into several sections with a sharp knife, being careful to have a root on each section. Each piece planted will form a new plant. Comfrey and angelica are also good candidates for this method.

DIVISIONS

When perennials begin to emerge in the spring, take a spade or garden fork and lift the plant for dividing. Separate the plant carefully making certain there are strong shoots and healthy roots on each section. Replant them immediately. Some herbs require dividing every three or four years to maintain a healthy plant.

LAYERING

Propagation by layering is the safest way of increasing your plants. The plant is never cut from the mother plant so it continues to be nourished until it has taken root on its own. Simply take a branch, bend it to the soil and place a stone or large bent wire on top of the stem. Cut a small opening in the underside of the stem where it touches the earth to encourage rooting. When the new roots form, the plant can be separated from the mother plant and set in its new location.

RUNNERS

Runners are very much like layering. Roots grow along some stems and when they come in contact with the soil a new plant is formed. Simply snip the new plant from the larger plant and move to an area of its own.

ANGELICA

Angelica archangelica
Hardy biennial (crafts, culinary, fragrance, medicinal, tea)
Zones 4-9

HISTORY

Since angelica originated in Greenland, Iceland and northern Russia, you would be correct if you think this plant can survive in cooler temperatures. It is hardy enough to have adapted well throughout Europe. It is said to bloom on the feast day of the Archangel Michael, May 8. This may well be the source of its name. But there are theorists who attribute the origin of the name to the legend of an angel giving the plant to man as a cure for plague. Ancient herbalists claimed angelica would cure some diseases, even protect against evil and witchcraft if you chewed the roots of the plant.

DESCRIPTION

Angelica, with its very lush growth, is a beautiful focal point in the garden. Growing as much as 8 feet tall, it should be placed at the back of the garden. It has stout, hollow stems that are purple at the base and presenting broad, lobed leaves which are 2 to 3 feet long, dividing into small, glossy, toothed leaflets. A relative of parsley and coriander, the blooms, which are even more spectacular, yellow-green and large, umbrella-like clusters, appear the second year in June or July. The honey-scented flowers put on a beautiful show and as all biennials do, then it dies. The flavor is sweet and licorice-like.

PLANTING AND PROPOGATION

Angelica does best when the soil is well-drained, cool, moist and rich. So plant where it will receive some shade and moisture. It also can be grown in deep pots. Purchase plants from nurseries. You can sow seeds, however, the seed is short-lived and must be planted immediately after it matures. The seeds need light to germinate, so sow uncovered in late summer, preferably where they will grow, since it's a poor transplanter. Thin to 3 feet apart.

Propagate with root cuttings or offshoots taken during the second year.

HARVESTING AND STORAGE

Small stems can be collected the first summer, then stems and leaves in the spring of the second year. The ripe seeds should be harvested before they shatter, dried and stored in air-tight containers in the refrigerator. Leaves which are collected can be frozen.

USES

This is a very sweet plant and all parts are used, but are best used fresh. Using only young stems, leaf stems can be candied and made into cake decorations. Leaves can be used in salads or cooked with fish or poultry; or toss fresh leaves into soups and stews. Seeds and the dry root can be infused and taken as a tea for relief from flatulence and as a tonic for colds. Seeds are used to flavor drinks, especially gin.

In potpourris, seeds act as a fixative. Or, in the spring make an incision at the crown to extract an aromatic gum, which is also used as a potpourri fixative. Leaves make

a great addition to potpourri mixtures.

Use crushed leaves to freshen the air in a car. They will also relieve travel sickness.

Use foliage in fresh floral arrangements.

ANISE

Pimpinella anisum
Tender annual (aromatic, culinary, medicinal)
Zones 4-9

HISTORY

A native of Egypt, Greece and the eastern Mediterranean, anise arrived in the United States during the 18th century, when settlers coming into Virginia were requested to bring and plant anise seeds. In the Orient, it is still widely used as a breath freshener. As early as the 11th century, the English scented their beds with sachets of anise. A valuable commodity, anise was a taxable item as it arrived on English docks, but was not cultivated there until the 16th century. It was soon discovered how dearly mice loved the anise scent and the English were soon placing it in mousetraps as bait.

The early Romans valued anise as a cough supressant and poison antidote, and it was highly regarded as a digestive curative. They even added the seeds to cakes which were served at weddings. This might have been the beginning of the traditional wedding cake as we know it today. Its main use through the centuries has been in flavoring drinks and liqueurs such as anisette and Pernod.

DESCRIPTION

A member of the carrot family, anise is a sweet, aromatic herb with a distinctive licorice flavor and bears a strong semblance to fennel. The flowers are small, creamy-white umbels similar to Queen Anne's lace, and bloom in July and August, followed by pale brown ribbed and flattened seeds. Its leaves are different as they go up the stem, with rounded basal leaves having serrated edges, and feathery, fine upper leaves. Anise oil contains insect-repellent properties, so very few pests bother this plant. Growing to a height of 1½ to 2 feet, anise makes a nice addition to any garden.

PLANTING AND PROPAGATION

Preferring a very warm climate, anise should be sown directly in a sunny spot after threat of all frosts. Plant seeds in a not-too-rich, light soil and provide generous and regular watering. Sow carefully since anise has a long taproot and does not transplant well. Be sure to mark the area as seeds are slow to germinate. It is very important to keep young plants well weeded. When 4 inches high, thin to 6 or 8 inches apart in rows 2 feet wide.

Anise is a good companion plant to coriander and planting them near each other will encourage both anise and coriander to perform well.

HARVESTING AND STORAGE

The leaves and seeds are both used from the anise plant, but since at least 4 frost-free months are required to grow seeds to maturity, the northern areas of the country can only harvest the leaves. Pick leaves

when fully mature and hang to dry. They can then be rolled between your palms to crumble for storage.

Gather seed heads when about one-half the crop has begun to turn brown. Cut stems just above ground level and tie in small bunches and hang in a dry, warm place until seeds are fully ripened. Rub off seeds, spread onto a tray, and dry for another week. Store tightly sealed in opaque containers. Snipping foliage as you need it only enhances the anise plant.

USES

Use leaves in salads and fish dishes, or with vegetables and mild cheeses. They are also good with sweet fruits, carrots, parsnips and yams. Anise is especially good with apples. Crush leaves and seeds. Use seeds as flavoring for sweet dishes, such as breads, cakes and candies. Be adventuresome and try anise in curry dishes. Try anise wherever you use cinnamon, nutmeg, cloves or allspice.

Crushed seeds added to sachets bring out the fragrance. Manufacturers use anise to enhance toothpastes and mouthwashes.

Long used to interest dogs in hunting foxes, the English dragged sacks containing the scent of anise along the ground to get the dogs to follow.

BASIL
Ocimum Basilicum
Annual (aromatic, culinary, ornamental)
Zones 3-10

HISTORY

To the French and Greek, this is the herb of kings; to the Italians, a gentle expression of love. Many cooks the world over, if given a vote for only one herb, would most likely choose basil as the "king of herbs." With its special affinity with tomatoes, basil has long been recognized as the "tomato herb." The discovery of using basil and tomatoes together is thought to have occurred by accident when cooks placed sprigs of basil over bowls of tomatoes to prevent flies from gathering.

Of course, all reviews are not so good. It has been said basil should be planted with cursing and screaming to guarantee a healthy plant and a healthy household. Some say from this came the expressions, "ranting and raving," and "seeding the basil." Superstitions surrounding basil include believing scorpions liked to hide under pots of basil and if you left a sprig under the pot it would turn into a scorpion.

DESCRIPTION

Basil is native to India and Asia and considered a perennial in those tropical climates. However, it's considered an annual in our climate. Growing to a height of about 2½ feet, its leafy stems lend it a bushy look. Its fragrant leaves have a peppery, clove-like scent which will permeate the garden, especially on a hot day. The leaves are 2 to 3

inches long, fleshy, and tend to curl. They are wrinkled and bright to dark green, depending on the richness of the soil. The plant sends forth spikes of whitish-purple, maybe even pink flowers, depending on the variety.

There are many basils: dark opal, mammoth, purple ruffles, Tulsi or sacred, miniature, Portuguese, Mexican, lemon, cinnamon and camphor, just to name a few. Many others are available and it's fun to experiment with them in the garden and in the kitchen.

PLANTING AND PROPAGATION

Basil is easily grown from seeds. To get an earlier start, you may wish to sow seeds indoors 6 weeks prior to the last expected frost. When plants are 3 to 4 inches tall, transplant them into a well-drained, rich soil. Plants are available at nurseries, but normally the more unusual varieties are available by seed only.

If starting basil by seed in the garden, sow in a sunny location after all danger of frost is past. Soil should be slightly warm, around 60°. Plant seeds ⅛ inch deep, thinning to 12 to 18 inches apart after seedlings appear.

Keep the plants pruned to encourage a bushy growth, and keep flowers plucked to promote and maintain leaf production, otherwise, energy will go to setting seeds and not to leaf production. Watering during dry spells is recommended as dry soil can stunt growth.

Basil is very sensitive to frost and will appear dark after touched by it. To prevent frost damage, cover with cloth or paper, not plastic.

Basil can be used as a companion plant to peppers and tomatoes to enhance their growth.

Propagation can be achieved quickly with young stem cuttings. Place in a glass of water and when several roots have begun to form, transplant to the garden.

HARVESTING AND STORAGE

Fresh basil is preferred; just pluck leaves as you need them. Harvest the tip foliage (or upper one-third of the plant) throughout the season to prevent flowering. Completely clean the plant of leaves prior to your frost date. Basil may be frozen or dried; however, some loss in quality may be experienced when dried.

To dry basil, cut stems prior to blooming by clipping the plant back to one-third its size. Place stems upside down in a paper bag and hang in a warm, dry area until dry. When dry, roll stems between your palms to crush and remove leaves. Save the stems and sprinkle onto the gray coals at your next cookout. Store the dried, crushed leaves in a tightly-sealed container.

To freeze, wash whole sprigs and store in freezer bags, expelling all air. It tastes as good as fresh!

USES

Well known as the tomato herb, basil leaves may be used in tomato-based dishes, tomato sauces, pesto sauce, soft cheeses and creamy sauces. Add it to lasagna and spaghetti, to salads, meats, baked fruits and fruit pies. Use basil sprigs, or even the flowers, for an attractive garnish. Basil is

great with eggs, beans, poultry, rice and fish and it blends well with garlic, thyme and lemons. Add the herb to garden vegetables such as potatoes, zucchini, carrots, squash or eggplant; however, add late in cooking as it loses flavor with long heating periods.

To obtain the most flavor from basil, shred the leaves with your hands instead of chopping with a knife.

Basil is said to aid digestion and stimulate appetites, so prepare plenty!

It's easy to prepare a basil butter (blend 1 tablespoon chopped basil with ½ cup butter) and brush on steaks or use to baste a roasted chicken. Add basil to scrambled eggs (1 teaspoon per 6 eggs).

Vinegars are wonderful flavored with basil. Use dark opal basil for an unusual colored vinegar or lemon basil for a very flavorful vinegar.

Basil can be used in bouquets with any cut flower arrangement. Its dried leaves are used in sachets and potpourri, adding a distinctly wonderful pungent aroma. For different fragrances, try lemon or cinnamon basil.

BAY, SWEET

Laurus nobilis
Perennial (aromatic, culinary, medicinal, ornamental)
Zones 4-10 (in containers)
Zones 9-10 (in open garden)

HISTORY

Laurus is the Latin term applied to the bay tree. It is native to the Mediterranean areas where laurel leaves were woven and used to crown the many heroes of Rome and Greece. The laurel tree was a sign of glory and honor. In 776 B.C., garlands of laurel were presented to the champions at the first Olympics.

In legend, Apollo, the Greek god of the sun, fell in love with the fair nymph, Daphne. However, Daphne would have nothing to do with him. In order to save Daphne from Apollo, her father changed her into a laurel tree. Apollo then declared the bay tree eternally sacred and thereafter wore a wreath of laurel leaves upon his head in her remembrance.

This is really a fabulous tree. According to legend, it protects you from thunder and lightning or witches and even the devil. It enjoys the reputation of helping with rheumatism, snakebites, wasp and bee stings, earaches and urinary problems. By the same token, the death of this tree was considered an evil omen.

There are numerous bay or laurel trees, however the sweet bay tree is the only one that is edible.

DESCRIPTION

Growing to heights of up to 10 feet in ground culture and 5 feet in potted culture, the bay is an evergeen perennial shrub having small shiny, deep green leaves which are very potent in essential oils. This plant is highly valued by cooks and wreath makers. It rarely flowers but when it does, the inconspicuous flowers are followed by dark purple or black one-seeded berries about the size of a small grape.

PLANTING AND PROPAGATION

Plant in full sun to partial shade in rich, well-drained soil. Bay grows well in the northern areas in pots but should be moved indoors for the winter. If purchasing plants, be sure to get the French bay and not the California bay, which by reputation has little flavor.

Cuttings can be taken from fresh green shoots in the fall and kept moist while trying to root. Rooting can take from 3 to 9 months. In warmer climates, sow seed outside and even then germination can take up to a year.

HARVESTING AND STORAGE

Collect and dry the leaves when needed for use or store in air-tight jars after drying. Leaves can be harvested at any time of the year. Dry the leaves in dark, cool conditions with a flat board on top of the leaves to prevent curling. It takes about 15 days to dry.

USES

The uses of bay are numerous but some are more useful than others. When cooking with bay, tear the edges prior to using for maximum flavor. Always remove from the dish before serving since the leaf is not palatable.

Use bay leaves to flavor soups, stews or keep in mind that if it requires simmering, it requires a bay leaf. The bay leaf is an important part of *bouquet garni*. Since it is a strong herb, it only takes one leaf to flavor a dish.

Use it when roasting game, meats or poultry. Add leaves to potato soup. Add bay to the charcoals when grilling fish. Use it when preparing vinegars. Just drop a leaf in!

Use a leaf when preparing marinades or add to herb salad dressings and let stand several hours for the flavoring to reach full potential before removing the leaf.

Sprinkle dried leaves throughout your kitchen cabinets to repel storage pests. Put a leaf or two in containers of flour or other grains to keep weevils out.

Use the leaves to make wreaths during the holidays.

When using bay leaves in dye making, a pale green dye will be produced.

CAUTION: All laurels with the exception of sweet bay are poisonous.

BEE BALM

Monarda didyma
Hardy perennial (culinary, medicinal, ornamental, tea)
Zones 4-9

HISTORY

The favorite drink of the Oswego Indians, who lived in what is now New York, came from the leaves of bee balm, sometimes called Oswego tea. Other common names are bergamot, golden melissa, Indian nettle and horsemint. The Indians used the plant to treat mild fevers, headaches, colds and sore throats.

The same plant helped the colonists fulfill their tea requirements after the Boston Tea Party in 1773 and all during the American Revolution. Native to eastern

North America, the colonists admired bee balm, not just for its use as a tea substitute during the period of time they couldn't get black tea, but for its beautiful red flowers.

DESCRIPTION

Easy to grow, bee balm gets to be as tall as 3 to 5 feet in shrub-like clumps. The plant has 6-inch, dark green, oval leaves, slightly toothed and hairy. The leaves emit a strong rich, orangy fragrance. The brilliant red flowers, which have a strong resemblance to mop heads, bloom from midsummer to fall. There are some varieties, including *Monarda fistulosa*, which produce pink to lavender flowers. All varieties attract bees, butterflies and hummingbirds. Bee balm is a member of the mint family and a particularly satisfying plant to have in your garden.

PLANTING AND PROPAGATION

Provide full sun, a moist, organic soil. If you live in a hot climate, provide partial shade. The easiest way to get started is to set transplants in the fall or spring, spacing plants 12 to 15 inches apart. Keep in mind young plants may take a season to bloom, so don't be discouraged if they do not bloom the first year. If they do try to blossom, cut the flower heads before they bloom the first summer to increase bloom size the following season. Propagate by dividing the clump in spring or fall.

Cut foliage back in the fall to within several inches of the ground and dig up every three years to divide and replant, which helps to control their rapid spread. Keep plants pinched back at the top to make them bushier. Harvesting flowers in the early summer will encourage more blooms later.

HARVESTING AND STORAGE

Pick flowers or leaves throughout the summer just prior to flowering when they are most fragrant. When the foliage becomes unattractive in late summer, harvest the leaves. Dry on drying trays or hang upside down by their stems.

USES

The attractive thing about this plant for flower arrangements is that the cut flowers are long lasting. The flowers are great for wreaths. Use fresh leaves or dried leaves in tea and potpourris. In cooking, leaves can be substituted for sage, but have a milder taste.

BORAGE

Borago officinalis
Annual (culinary, ornamental, tea)
Zones 3-9

HISTORY

Native to the Mediterannean area, borage has long been associated with courage and good cheer. This may be true, since it is high in potassium (in the form of nitrate of potash) which is known to stimulate the adrenal glands, thereby creating the semblance of courage. To inspire bravery, borage was incorporated into the patterns of the scarves which ladies presented to knights for battle wear.

Ancient Celtic warriors, prior to battle, drank wine flavored with borage to give them courage. As their fears disap-

peared, elation would occur. Borage received the credit for this elation, not the wine. John Evelyn, a 17th century diarist, encouraged the use of borage sprigs in wine "to revive the hypochondriac and cheer the hard student."

DESCRIPTION

Borage grows 1 to 3 feet tall with large, fuzzy leaves. Its bright sky-blue, star-shaped flowers, which hang in drooping clusters on the plant, appear in mid-summer. The blue green oval leaves have a distinct cucumber taste. The plant attracts bees and butterflies with its abundance of nectar and pollen. This plant gives a great deal of pleasure just seeing the swirl of blue star flowers in your garden.

PLANTING AND PROPAGATION

Borage is quick to grow from seed and is self-seeding. It may become a pest, but probably a pest you'll appreciate. It tolerates poor soil but prefers porous, alkaline soil and desires full to partial sun. Keep soil moist and free from competing weeds by using a mulch.

Plant seeds about 20 to 24 inches apart once soil warms in spring. Any transplanting should be done when the plants are small.

Borage makes a good companion plant to strawberries, increasing their production.

HARVESTING AND STORAGE

The preferred method of storage for borage is in vinegar. However, the flowers can be frozen in ice cube trays. Simply freeze ⅓ cube of ice, then place a flower on top, fill the remainder of the cube with water, and freeze. Borage cubes make wonderful additions to teas and other iced drinks.

USES

Toss fresh borage flowers in salads or garnish foods with them. Candy the flowers and leaves and use to decorate cakes and cookies. The leaves can be cooked as greens (the fine, bristly hairs dissipate with cooking). Borage leaves are very pleasing scattered over a dish of tomatoes in vinaigrette.

CALENDULA

Calendula officinalis
Annual (culinary, dye, medicinal, ornamental)
Zones 3-9

HISTORY

India is thought to be the originating point of calendula, but it is native from the Canary Islands through southern and central Europe and even North Africa. Used by the Romans for treating scorpion bites, they also are given credit for the naming. Observing that the flowers opened on the first day of *calends* of every month, they named it calendula. The calendar developed by the Romans evidently shares a kinship with calendula. Chaucer called the blossom "yellow Goldes" and the monks referred to them as "Mary-goldes." One of its more common names is "pot marigold."

Medicinally, calendula is considered to be anti-inflammatory, astringent, antiseptic, and cooling. It inhibits bleeding and is thought to stimulate new skin growth.

DESCRIPTION

Growing to a height of 12 to 24 inches and spreading to 12 inches, calendula makes a wonderful potted plant and a garden plant for fresh bouquets. Thin to 9 or 10 inches apart. The plant blooms all summer and into the fall and even after the first frost with bright, orange flowers blooming on sturdy stems which hold the large pale, green leaves. The daisy-like flowers will close at night and even on very cloudy days, then open up to greet the morning sun. This plant will survive frosts and even early snows.

Calendula is not saffron, but simmering petals will produce an orange-colored liquid similar to saffron and is suitable for flavoring dishes.

PLANTING AND PROPAGATION

Calendula will grow almost anywhere, but prefers the sun and a little dappled shade and a rich, loamy soil. Seed can be sown in autumn or spring directly into the garden. After the first season, it will happily reseed itself. When it becomes too hot, the plants will begin to wane, but don't give up on them. Simply cut them back about two-thirds and they will revive when it cools a bit.

HARVESTING AND STORAGE

Dry petals by removing from the blossoms and spreading them on dry paper. Grind them to a powder and store in an air tight container. Petals retain their golden color when dried, which makes them a good candidate for potpourris.

USES

Substitute calendula petals when you require saffron, especially in rice, potpourris and skin preparations. Use petals in wine punches, cheeses, and to add a gourmet touch, toss into salads or soups. Add to your bath water and cut fresh calendula for floral arrangements. Use plants liberally in your garden. They make a beautiful feature and with the newer varieties, an even wider range of color is available, from creamy yellow to brilliant orange.

CARAWAY

Carum carvi
Biennial (culinary)
Zones 3-5

HISTORY

Native to the Middle East, Asia, and central Europe, caraway has been used for more than 5000 years, as suggested by food remnants found among Mesolithic digs. Used by Scandinavian countries more than any other countries, caraway is used as a seasoning in breads such as rye and pumpernickel. Caraway is included in dumplings, cheeses, noodle dishes and goulashes and added to coleslaw, sauerkraut and even liqueurs. Flavoring cookies and cakes with caraway has long been practiced.

DESCRIPTION

Since caraway is a member of the

parsley family, it's no surprise the taste is similar. It is also a relative of fennel and dill. It grows 1½ to 2 feet tall and spreads about 8 inches wide. The first year of caraway is spent producing foliage and it will bring forth beautiful white umbel blossoms in the second year to produce its wonderful seeds. The leaves are finely-cut and resemble carrot foliage. Seeds are small, oval, and ribbed light to dark brown in color.

PROPAGATION AND PLANTING

Sow caraway seed outdoors in late April or early May in a not-too-rich soil, or it will produce a lot of foliage and fewer seeds. Prepare the soil with a good general clean-up, level it and dampen with water. When the soil is workable, prepare small furrows or grooves 10 inches apart and ⅛-inch deep. Sprinkle seed evenly and cover lightly with soil, firming it around the seeds. Keep the soil moist until the seeds begin to sprout, then thin to 10 inches apart. Excessive pruning during the first year will weaken the plant. During the second season pinch flower stalks as they develop to encourage the plant to live another season.

HARVESTING AND STORAGE

Since caraway is a biennial, it will concentrate on developing the first year and produce seeds for harvesting in the second season. The seeds are ripe when they turn brown. They can be collected by cutting the entire plant and hanging it upside down in a paper bag to collect the dropping seeds.

USES

Caraway has the ability to cross over in cooking from sweets and savory foods. Fresh leaves can be chopped into a salad, much the same as parsley. Its seeds are wonderful in breads, cakes, soups and stews. Chew on a few seeds after eating garlic to cleanse your breath.

As the Germans and Austrians do, add it to sauerkraut, potatoes and seed cakes. Add it to beef, cheeses and fish. The root can be used just as you would a parsnip in soups and stews.

CATMINT/CATNIP

Nepeta cataria
Hardy perennial (crafts, culinary, ornamental)
Zones 4-8

HISTORY

Medicinally dating back more than 2000 years to a Europe where catnip tea was regularly consumed, catnip was used for colds and cold symptoms and helping colicky babies. It was brought to America by the colonists for medicinal use and for their mildly hallucinogenic dried leaves. Since eating catnip would make people quarrelsome, hangmen would eat it to give them the courage to carry out their duties.

Catnip was mentioned in the writings of Washington Irving, Nathaniel Hawthorne and even Harriet Beecher Stowe. The name catnip is usually limited to *N. cataria* with catmint referring to most all the other species.

It has been observed that if you set a transplant of catnip, you will probably

bruise the leaves, thereby attracting cats to this plant. However, if you sow seeds, cats will probably never bother the plants.

DESCRIPTION

A member of the mint family with square stems, catnip is a vigorous grower, with heart-shaped, downy, gray-green leaves. Crush a catnip leaf and a volatile oil, nepetalactone, concentrated in glands on the surface of the leaves, will permeate the air. This supposed hallucinogen is what cats crave. Kittens do not seem to react to this oil as much as the older cats do, but even then not all cats react.

The 2-to-3-foot tall plant often spreads as wide as it is tall. Its flowers are white with purple-pink dots and bloom July through September. It has a mild lemony mint flavor and when flavored with honey is recommended for hyperactive children, as well as for insomnia, headaches, fever and indigestion in adults.

PLANTING AND PROPAGATION

Locate plants in full sun or partial shade, preferably in rich soil. Plant in the early spring by sowing seeds or with transplants from a friend or a nursery. This plant spreads easily, so seedlings will be available to increase the number of plants in your garden. Thin to 18 inches apart. After flowering, cut off plants to 4 to 8 inches high encouraging another bloom period. Propagate from cuttings placed directly in the soil.

HARVESTING AND STORAGE

Gather bunches of catnip leaves just before they are in full bloom and hang them upside down in a well-ventilated room or spread on trays. When the leaves rustle, remove them from the stems and store in an air-tight container. An autumn shearing will keep catnip trim and happy.

USES

Fresh leaves can be candied by dipping into a mixture of beaten egg white and lemon juice; sprinkling each side with sugar and letting dry for a day or so. Store in a tightly-closed container in the refrigerator.

Make a relaxing tea from the leaves.

Leaves make great stuffing for cat toys. Simply stuff a tiny sock and toss to your kitty.

Catnip plants will attract bees. The plants are bushy enough to make an attractive edging to your garden.

CHAMOMILE

Chamaemelum nobile (Roman)
Perennial (aromatic, cosmetic, tea)
Zones 3-8

HISTORY

For all the people who read Beatrix Potter's *Peter Rabbit* when they were young, this herb will bring back fond memories of the "one tablespoonful" of chamomile tea his mother dosed him with after a very difficult day. Chamomile is a Greek word meaning "ground apple." One of the favorite herbs in medieval gardens, chamomile was believed to keep all other plants healthy.

It is native to the Mediterranean area and found in most of western Europe.

The Egyptians dedicated chamomile to the sun and raised it for its healing abilities. It was sometimes smoked to cure insomnia and the relaxing apple aroma affected all who were around it. In folk medicine, chamomile is a "children's plant," due to its many uses for children's problems.

DESCRIPTION

A relative of the sunflower and growing to a height of 9 to 12 inches with a spread of 4 to 6 inches, chamomile's fine-leaved stems and small stature at first appear to be ferns. It has a bright green color and daisy-like flowers. Eventually it spreads by means of underground shoots to form a solid ground cover that can be mowed about 3 inches high.

Roman chamomile is a perennial and can be identified by the flower's flat, solid center. German is an annual which can be recognized by the hollow, conical yellow center in the flower. Dyer's chamomile has long blooming bright yellow flowers.

PLANTING AND PROPAGATION

Hardy to -20°F, chamomile is an evergreen, commonly used as lawns in England. It is spread by underground shoots. Plant by sowing seed or with transplants in early spring, or by division in spring or fall. Chamomile should be planted in full sun in average to poor soil with good drainage. It will take some shade, but really prefers the sun. It needs to be planted in groups since one plant is too small for any effect. Plant 4 to 6 inches apart for the quickest effect. During the first year, keep clipped to promote growth of its foliage.

HARVESTING AND STORAGE

Whole plants can be harvested at any time or when the flowers are fully open. Dry by hanging. Air dry the flowers on a screen and use them in tea. Store in air-tight containers.

USES

To make chamomile tea, steep 1 tablespoon of fresh blossoms in 1 cup of boiling water for 5 minutes and then srain. Fresh or dried German chamomile blossoms can be used. It is soothing and relaxing, especially if you suffer from insomnia. Its sweet flavor is a favorite with children as well.

Boil flowers for 20 minutes and use as a rinse to lighten and condition fair hair.

Use chamomile in potpourri and herb pillows or in your bath to relieve sunburn or windburn.

CHERVIL

Anthriscus cerefolium
Annual (culinary, medicinal)
Zones 3-7

HISTORY

Native to Europe and Asia, chervil was believed to improve humor, jolt the memory and restore youth. At one time it was believed curing the hiccups could be achieved simply by eating an entire chervil plant. It also has an aroma resembling myrrh, a gift to Baby Jesus. As a result, believing chervil symbolizes new life, it became common to serve chervil soup on Maundy Thursday.

DESCRIPTION

Chervil is a small plant, 12 to 18 inches tall, much like parsley and with lacy, indented leaves. An annual, having tiny white flowers on umbels, chervil is sometimes called French parsley or Gourmet's parsley and is one of the ingredients in fines herbes along with parsley, chives and tarragon. Chervil has a taste similar to Italian parsley with just a hint of anise. Since only its leaves are used, chervil is treated as an annual, although technically it is a biennial.

PLANTING AND PROPAGATION

If summers are cool, plant chervil in a sunny location; plant in a partially-shaded location if in a hot climactic area. Chervil prefers a slightly shady location and makes a good container plant. Seeding is the best means of planting because it transplants poorly. Since chervil needs light to germinate, sow seeds in a 1-inch furrow without covering and lightly mist the seeds. Indoors, chervil can be started from seed in a pot. It self sows freely if allowed to flower.

HARVESTING AND STORAGE

Only the leaves of chervil are used. To promote foliage, pinch the flowers off as soon as they appear. Apply liquid fertilizer regularly. Successive plantings should be made during the season, as chervil is fast to bolt.

Young leaves harvested as early as 6 to 8 weeks will be the most flavorful. Chervil can be frozen or dried for storage. It loses some of its flavor, however, by drying. Another good method of preserving flavor is making chervil butter and freezing it until needed.

USES

Chervil's greatest value is its culinary use. It's the delicate ingredient in *fines herbes* (for omelettes) and the key ingredient of béarnaise sauce and vinaigrette. Add it to butter to baste or to a sauce to accompany chicken or fish. Always add just before serving, since the flavor dissipates quickly. It can be used as a substitute for Italian parsley.

CHIVES

Allium schoenoprasum
Perennial (culinary, ornamental)
Zones 3-9

HISTORY

Chives have had a culinary use for nearly 5000 years. Native to the Orient, chives found its way to Europe and was later brought to America by the early settlers. At one time, it was believed chives could prevent evil influences and diseases, so chives were hung in the home for protection.

DESCRIPTION

The common chive is a bulb plant and the smallest member of the amaryllis or onion family of shallots, garlic, and onions. It multiplies fast and grows very thick, with round hollow grass-like leaves growing into a taper. The plants will grow to a height of 12 to18 inches, with a stem appearing in summer producing papery lavender umbel flowers, resembling clover blossoms. Both the blossoms and leaves are edible.

PLANTING AND PROPAGATION

Chives prefer a rich soil in a sunny location and will germinate slowly, requiring darkness and constant moisture at a temperature of 60°-70°F. Sow the seeds half-inch deep in flats of soil mix. When seedlings are four weeks old they can be transplanted into the garden. If allowed to flower, chives will reseed themselves from the small, black seeds found in the flower head in late summer. Chives should be divided every 3 to 4 years in order to prevent disease and overcrowding.

HARVESTING AND STORAGE

The leaves can be clipped anytime after they are 6 inches tall, cutting to within 2 inches of the ground. If cut higher, they will begin to look ragged. Never cut all the leaves since some leaves are required for furnishing nutrients to the bulbs.

Chives are easily stored by freezing in ice cubes. Cut several leaves, chop or snip, and place in icetrays with water and freeze. Remove and store in freezer bags to use as needed.

Use flowers in vinegars and maybe toss a few in your salad.

USES

Tasting like mild, sweet onions, chives are best known for their culinary adaptations and can be used in any dish which calls for onions. Chives can be used as a garnish for vegetables, such as squash, beans, tomatoes, and salads. They are often put in soups, egg and cheese dishes, herb butters, cottage cheese and cream cheese. Always add chives to cooking during the last few minutes.

Freeze chive butter in a plastic wrap and slice as needed for baked potatoes, hot breads, biscuits and even vegetables.
Try combining chunks of cucumber, ripe tomato and feta cheese with minced fresh chives. Add a splash of olive oil and serve with crusty bread.

Chives are also pretty enough to use as a border anywhere in your gardens. They do not allow weeds to invade them. Around roses, they help prevent black spot and repel carrot flies around carrots.

CONEFLOWER

Echinacea angustifolia
Perennial (medicinal, ornamental)
Zones 4-8

HISTORY

From the Greek word *echinos* meaning hedgehog, comes the name echinacea. This references the plant's prickly seed heads. Native Americans used coneflower extensively, calling it by several names, some of which are snakeroot, rattlesnake weed and scurvy root. They used the roots to treat numerous problems, including burns and snake bites as the nicknames indicate. They also used the fresh juice of the herb to desensitize their feet before fire walking rituals over hot coals.

Coneflower is a popular remedy for colds and flu, as it stimulates the immune system and directly attacks viruses. This herb speeds the healing of wounds and speeds the recovery period from viruses.

DESCRIPTION

Coneflower, a perennial, is native to North American prairies. It is found on grasslands, open woods and on roadsides. These are vigorous perennials with dark green foliage and striking flowers which could range anywhere from white to purple and reds and yellows. Along with the prickly seed head, which is distinctly conical in shape, the purple petals remind you of a badminton shuttlecock.

It can grow as tall as 4 feet with a daisy-like flower. It blooms early summer and into early autumn. Coneflower is a member of the daisy family and is drought tolerant. You can simply enjoy the beautiful blooms in your garden. It works well in perennial and cut flower gardens as well as the herb garden.

PLANTING AND PROPAGATION

Sow seed in ordinary, well-manured garden soil in late spring or early summer after the soil has warmed up (70°F) in a sunny location. Or divide existing purple coneflowers in April. Keep the fading flowers snipped to encourage continual blossoming. Coneflower can tolerate hot, dry summers and can withstand cold to 30°F below zero. Providing mulch around the plants during the winter months will certainly ensure their return in the spring.

HARVESTING AND STORAGE

Parts used are the rootstock. Wait until after the plant has experienced several hard frosts and begins to die back before digging for the root. It can then be cleaned and dried. The crown of the plant can be replanted after the root has been harvested, but this harvesting will cause the plant to be weakened medicinally.

USES

This plant is loved by all including the bees and butterflies. It is a plus for your garden as a cut flower for bouquets. Even the seed heads are used in crafts. Leaving the plants standing during the winter months will attract birds when the snows fall.

CORIANDER

(Cilantro)
Coriandrum sativum
Annual (aromatic, culinary)
Zones 2-9

HISTORY

Coriander, prior to maturity, has a strong unpleasant smell some compare to the smell of bedbugs. The name comes from the Greek word, *koros*, meaning bedbug.

Dating back to biblical times, it earned its place in many societies, among which were the Romans, who used it as a preservative, and by the Egyptians as a funeral offering. The Hebrews used it as one of the bitter herbs in the ritual of the Passover. The seed was compared to manna which was sent from heaven to feed the Israelites. The Chinese believed it had the power to make a person immortal.

DESCRIPTION

Coriander, a member of the parsley family, is a bright green annual, growing to

1½ feet or more. The seeds, coriander, of this plant are used to flavor confections, soups and alcoholic beverages. A hardy annual, this plant produces two types of leaves.

The bottom leaves, cilantro, are similar to Italian parsley in looks. However, they have a much stronger aroma that is becoming very fashionable. The lemony taste is one you either love or hate. Used in southwestern dishes, cilantro can be added to salads and salsas for an extra zing.

The top leaves, being very fine, are not used for cooking. The plant bears tiny pink or lavender flowers in the summer, followed by the round fruits, each producing a seed. When mature, the seeds take on a spicy, orange fragrance.

PLANTING AND PROPAGATION

In spring, sow seeds in rows one foot apart in a sunny spot after all danger of frost. Seeds can be sown in the fall, if the winters are mild. Plant in a well-drained, ordinary soil, since rich, moist soils produce less-than-desirable plants and seeds that lack flavor and aroma. For a steady supply of fresh foliage, make successive sowings every 3 to 4 weeks through fall. The plant has a deep taproot, so plant where they will stay. Coriander is a prolific self-seeder.

Coriander is a very good companion plant to dill, however, do not grow it near fennel as it often prevents fennel seeds from forming.

HARVESTING AND STORAGE

When these fruits or seeds, which have an edible inner seed, are ripened to a brownish grey, clip the seed head a short way down the stem, place in a paper bag and put in a well-ventilated place to dry. In 5 or 6 days the round fruit husks should be dry and will split into two halves, allowing the edible inner seed to drop out. Seeds should be scalded to protect them from insects during storage. Store in a tightly-sealed container.

The leaves should be used fresh. Flavor is lost when stored for any length of time. Freezing is used to preserve the cilantro leaves for future use.

USES

The green leaves, known as cilantro or Chinese parsley, are best when used fresh, since they lose flavor when dried. Fresh leaves are wonderful in salads and salsas and bring a special touch to fish and poultry. For poultry, crush fresh sage, cilantro and dill with a mortar and pestle; rub mixture over a lightly oiled chicken before roasting.

The seeds are used ground or whole in baking or with cooked fruit and in curries. The flavor of coriander and cilantro is strong, so use it in moderation when adding to any food. Try it in guacamole or in stir-fried food. The coriander plant is a staple in the diet of Mexicans, Chinese and the Indians. The seeds are used commercially in sausage and gin. They can also be added to potpourri for a lemony scent.

DILL

Anethum graveolens
Annual (aromatic, culinary, medicinal, ornamental)
Zones 2-9

HISTORY

Visually, dill is one of the most pleasing herbs in any garden. Watching it, gracefully swaying as the wind blows is relaxing and hypnotic, which explains how it got its Norse name, dilla, meaning "to lull." At one time it was used as a sleep agent. An ancient plant, it was believed to work as a milk stimulant for nursing mothers and as a charm against witches! Tiny pillows filled with dill were made to place under the heads of infants to lull them to sleep in their nurseries.

Dill was added to love potions, as well as to wine, to encourage passion.

DESCRIPTION

A hardy annual, which will reseed itself over a widespread area, dill grows to a height of 2 to 4 feet. Both members of the parsley family, dill is very similar to fennel, having hollow stems, feathery blue-green leaves, and umbels of greenish-yellow flowers, which later form brown, aromatic seeds. As with coriander, dill is grown for both its seed and leaves, the latter referred to as dillweed.

PLANTING AND PROPAGATION

Dill makes a wonderful addition to any vegetable, flower or herb garden. It is a tall plant, so it works well in the back of a flower or herb garden. In the vegetable garden, it keeps watch over cabbages to protect them from the white cabbage butterfly. It's thought to enhance the growth of onions and lettuce, but do not plant near carrots. Plant dill where it will receive some protection from winds or stake the plants for added support.

Full sun and rich, well-drained soil are preferable. Sow seeds directly in the spring soil, 2 to 4 weeks before the last expected frost, and rake lightly. Keep the surface evenly moist until the plants are established. For a constant supply of fresh dillweed, sow every 2 weeks. Thin seedlings 3 to 4 inches apart. Seedlings do not transplant well and dill begun from transplants tends to go to seed quickly without producing much foliage.

HARVESTING AND STORAGE

Dill can be harvested anytime from seedling stage until bloom by clipping leaves close to the stem. Foliage is most aromatic just before the flowers begin to open. Dillweed will only keep a couple of days in the refrigerator before it begins to droop and lose its flavor. The leaves can be frozen in a bag but be sure to press out excess air. When needed, simply snip some off with scissors and return the rest to the freezer. Dill dries well simply by hanging. Wrap a rubber band around a bundle of stems and as the dill dries and shrinks the rubber band will adjust to the shrinkage.

Harvest the seeds when seeds on the underside of the umbel are browning. The others will ripen as they dry. Hang over a basket or paper bag to catch the seeds as they fall.

USES

The spicy, anise-flavored leaves can be used in soups, stews, fish sauces and breads. It is delicious with vegetables and widely used in making pickles. You may wish to sprinkle a few leaves over a salad, or mix it with cream cheese or sour cream for a wonderful dip for vegetables. To make dill vinegar, steep a seed head and part of the stem in 1 pint of vinegar and put in a jar. Strain after 2 weeks.

Dill umbels can be dried and used with wreaths, or fresh, in flower arrangements. It gives any arrangement a light, airy feeling. I have used dill umbels as a delicate addition to my Christmas tree for several years.

FENNEL

Foeniculum vulgare
Semi-hardy Perennial (aromatic, cosmetic, culinary, medicinal, ornamental, tea)
Zones 6-9

HISTORY

The Greeks called it *marathon,* meaning "to grow thin." The British herbalist, Culpeper, wrote that all parts of fennel "are much used in drink or broth to make people lean who are too fat." The seeds were widely used as an appetite suppressant. In the Middle Ages it was used as a strewing herb. Not only did it smell good, it also kept insects away. It was believed to restore color to pale skin and improve eyesight. The Romans called it *foenum*, the Latin word for hay, which refers to its hay-like smell.

DESCRIPTION

Fennel, a member of the parsley family, is similar in appearance to dill. Growing 3 to 5 feet tall, its filigreed leaves are on tall, round, hollow stems that are thick and fleshy at the base. Dense, light green foliage gradually picks up a bluish tinge as the plant matures. Yellow flowers, in flat-topped clusters up to 6 inches wide, bloom in late summer and early fall producing light tan seeds. It has a taste close to that of licorice and is grown for its seeds, leaves and stems. This makes a beautiful, lush planting in any garden.

PLANTING AND PROPAGATION

Plant fennel in full sun to partial shade, in a well-drained soil after all danger of frost. Fennel will shade other herbs, so place it near herbs that need shade. Do not plant near coriander, as they will inhibit each other's growth. Avoid planting it near dill, since cross pollination could occur. Like dill, fennel does not transplant well. Plant seeds ½ inch deep, and thin to 8 inches apart. Once established, fennel is quite drought resistant.

HARVESTING AND STORAGE

Fennel leaves can be harvested anytime after reaching a height of about 6 inches. Harvest seeds as they ripen. If left on the plant to ripen, it will reseed itself. When the seeds begin to turn brown, cut off the umbel and place in a paper bag and hang in a well-ventilated area to dry. After drying, simply powder them and store in air-tight containers. Fennel also freezes well. Fresh cuttings will keep about a week in the refrigerator if

stems are placed in water.

The variety, Florence fennel or Finocchio, is a dwarf type grown mostly for the false bulb that is eaten like a vegetable, either cooked or raw. This selection grows only 1 to 2 feet tall. For a milder taste, blanch the bulbs prior to planting. This in turn makes them more tender. After planting, when the bulbs are about the size of eggs, mound the soil around the base of the plants. They can be harvested when about 3 inches in diameter.

USES

Being an appetite suppressor, fennel is obviously the herb for dieters. Tea made from fennel leaves can help curb hunger and do it deliciously. To make tea, pour ½ pint of boiling water over a teaspoon of bruised seeds.

Mix fennel with melted butter and serve over fish or lay some dried stalks over the grill while cooking fish; it adds a nice, subtle flavor. Fennel adds flavor to breads, cookies, soups and tomato sauces. Toss some of the seeds into your next tuna salad. Its seeds are a good substitute for a breath freshener. The plant is believed to cure a number of ills and ward off witches, as well.

FEVERFEW

Chrysanthemum parthenium
Perennial/Hardy biennial (culinary, medicinal, ornamental)
Zones 5-7

HISTORY

Feverfew is a native of southeast Europe and has naturalized elsewhere in Europe and in North America where it is found in woods edges. It was first recommended in 1633 by British herbalist Gerard for use as a headache remedy. It has since been suggested as a remedy in preventing and reducing migraines. With its cumulative effect in slowly reducing the muscle spasms implicated in migraines, the herb was used widely for relief and is now once again enjoying a new surge of popularity.

It was planted around European cottages to discourage disease and as an insect repellent.

DESCRIPTION

Feverfew is a member of the chrysanthemum family. It grows with a branched and tufted root. Even though the center of its blossom is flat, it is sometimes confused with chamomile which has a dome-shaped center. The leaves of the feverfew plant are strong and bitter scented. The flower stems are 4 inches long with daisy-like white blossoms.

Growing to a height of 1 to 3 feet and a width of 1 to 2 feet, feverfew will self-seed profusely. Trim the flowers back once they bloom to encourage another blooming period.

PLANTING AND PROPAGATION

Sow seed in a sunny area in the spring after all danger of frost, or in autumn. Provide a well-drained location avoiding wet areas. Thin or transplant to 9 to 12 inches apart. In late summer propagate by taking stem cuttings or start new plants from divisions made in spring or fall. Plant in a location whereyou do not want bees. They hate the smell of feverfew.

HARVESTING AND STORAGE

Flowers and leaves can be dried anytime. After drying, store in an air-tight container. Leaves can be frozen and stored in a plastic bag in the freezer.

USES

The leaves of feverfew can be added to small amounts of food to "cut" the fat. Add flowers to potpourri for color. Feverfew makes an excellent cut flower and low-growing varieties work beautifully in rock gardens or window boxes.

Fresh leaves and stems produce a greenish-yellow dye.

FLAX

Linum usitatissimum
Hardy Annual (fibers, medicinal, oil, ornamental)
Zones 4-9

HISTORY

In mythology, flax was said to be protected by the goddess Hulda, who taught mortals the art of growing, spinning and weaving flax. During the Middle Ages, flax flowers were considered a protection against sorcery. Egyptians wrapped their mummies in flax cloth and decorated their tombs with carvings of flax. Christ was wrapped in a flax cloth when placed in his tomb.

Bohemians believed that if children danced among flax at the age of 7 they would become beautiful.

Flax is a major farm crop in Russia, Canada and in the northern plains states of America. It is used for fine papers and is grown for the linseed oil it produces.

Producing linen required soaking flax in water, drying in the sun, binding in bundles, knocking and beating until in fibers, then spun. A fabric produced in the early colonial days of America, called linsey-woolsey, was very durable and made and worn by slaves of that time.

DESCRIPTION

Growing 1 to 4 feet tall with narrow, hairy sword-shaped leaves and erect stems which branch off at the top with red, white or blue flowers having five petals, flax blooms in late spring to early summer. Later capsules with light brown shiny seeds which are high in oils with linoleic acid appear. This plant is a pleasure early in the morning, but the hot sun takes its toll and causes it to wither slightly, only to appear freshly revived the next morning.

PLANTING AND PROPAGATION

In the spring, plant seeds in a sunny location with well-drained soil. When weeding, be careful not to pull out the shallow-rooted flax. After the plant is full-grown,

apply fertilizer. Allow the soil to dry between waterings.

HARVESTING AND STORAGE

Harvest just before the flowers bloom. Leave the seeds to ripen on the cut stems (sheaths) or let them mature on the plant after the blossoms drop. Keep the seeds dry. Dampness will damage them.

USES

Flax can be used in weaving baskets. Flax is used primarily as an ornamental plant in the herb garden. Formerly used medicinally as a cough and cold remedy, it is also known as linseed. Seed oil is important in paint and varnish manufacturing and in the making of linoleum. Stems are important for making paper and cloth. The fibers provide linen when spun. Flax seeds are also used in bread making.

CAUTION: Immature seedpods are especially poisonous, but all parts contain toxins. Use with caution.

GARLIC

Allium sativum
Perennial (culinary, medicinal)
Zones 5-10

HISTORY

Far East records show garlic dating back to 2000 B.C. Garlic was consumed by the Israelites in the wilderness. Slaves ate garlic during the building of the pyramids to maintain strength and endurance, with his-

tory recording they refused to work when garlic was removed from their diet.

Garlic is given medicinal credit throughout the centuries for its use in treating many ailments. Herbalists of ancient Far East treated high blood pressure and respiratory problems with garlic. Some herbalists have used it to treat colds and toothaches. In the infancy of our country, doctors used it as a disinfectant. It was applied to wounds during World War I and World War II to prevent septic poisoning and gangrene.

Garlic is known for its ability to lower cholesterol and prevent blood clots from forming.

It was believed to possess magical powers against evil, with folklore describing necklaces of garlic used by the superstitious to deter vampires. This probably kept more than vampires at a distance.

DESCRIPTION

A member of the lily family, garlic is an onion with a compound bulb made up of 8 to 12 cloves. Each clove has a papery covering with the whole bulb being enclosed in a white skin. Its flat, iris-like leaves rise from the bulbous base up to 2 feet tall, with very small, pinkish, star-shaped flowers appearing in the summer. The taste is a pungent, strong one, but well worth it.

PLANTING AND PROPAGATION

Planting garlic is easy. Simply separate one head of fresh garlic into cloves and plant them pointed end up in full sun and in a sandy, rich soil. Plant about 2 inches deep and leave 4 to 6 inches between plants. Plant in early spring 6 weeks before the last frost in

order to harvest in the fall, or you can plant cloves in late summer for harvesting the next year in spring or early summer. When the flower stalk appears, clip it off so the plant will direct its energy to producing a larger bulb.

HARVESTING AND STORAGE

You can begin harvesting when the leaves begin to wither and turn yellow. Its leaves can be braided and hung in a dry place for slow drying of the bulbs. Or, as some recommend, use a nylon stocking to store the bulbs. Twist off the dried leaves and drop bulbs into the stocking, tying a knot between each bulb. When you need a garlic bulb, simply snip one off just below the knot.

USES

Scientists are studying garlic today as being beneficial in the treatment of mild diabetes, diarrhea, hepatitis, whooping cough, typhoid, diptheria and dysentery. It has been suggested that garlic is helpful in lowering cholesterol levels and thinning blood. It is possible that garlic can help prevent cancers of the esophagus, colon, breast and stomach.

Garlic's main use is in cooking. It blends with most foods and has become a common, necessary item on today's kitchen shelves in the forms of fresh garlic, garlic salt and garlic powder.

Garlic has a pungent flavor, so use discretion. In cooking, it is commonly used with parsley which tends to mellow it. Most Italian and French recipes call for garlic but it is appreciated similarly around the globe.

I've heard it stated, "I love anything with garlic in it." Could be that it's habit forming.

To break the skin of a clove of garlic, smash it gently with a cleaver or large knife. To prevent a bitter taste, be careful not to brown or burn it during cooking. As a measure, the longer garlic cooks the milder it becomes.

Use garlic in soups, butters, sauces and stuffings. Use it when cooking meats, fish and poultry. Add garlic to herb vinegars. Some dishes, such as pesto, tomato sauce and most eggplant dishes cry out for garlic. Spread garlic butter on French bread.

Some people consider the odor of garlic as a social drawback, but it doesn't have to be. Mask the garlic smell on your breath by chewing on fresh parsley, which contains chlorophyl, or chew on a coffee bean or a fennel sprig. To remove the scent from your hands, rub them with lemon, then salt; rinse and wash with warm soapy water. Or dip your fingers in vinegar!

Garlic is a wonderful companion plant to roses, to deter aphids, and to eggplants, tomatoes and fruit trees.

GERMANDER

Teucrium
Perennial (crafts, ornamental)
Zones 5-9

HISTORY

In medieval times, this perennial herb was believed to help cure gout and improve the mind. Germander provided a

lot of pleasure to the Elizabethans when they designed knot gardens to include this herb, which was sometimes called "poor man's boxwood." With its evergreen, glossy leaves, it helped to define their garden shapes. George Washington is said to have fully appreciated germander because he could walk outdoors in February to find the glossy green leaves spangled with a coat of frost.

DESCRIPTION

There are as many as 100 varieties of germander. It grows 1 to 2 feet tall and the same in width. It flowers from July to September with tiny pink blooms providing a beautiful focal point in the herb garden. It's an evergreen in Zone 7 and the South. However, in Zones 5 and 6, it dies back to the ground in winter but appears again in the early spring. It has small toothed green leaves.

Some varieties have greenish-gray oval leaves and small, creamy white blossoms. Foliage of germander is lightly aromatic sometimes called "garliclike."

PLANTING AND PROPAGATION

Plant in full sun with some partial shade in average soil, but well-drained. This plant will adapt well to any garden condition as long as it is not situated in dampness. Begin germander with transplants since it grows so slowly from seed. Propagate by cuttings and layering. Divisions can be taken in the fall. North of Zone 7, mulching is recommended.

HARVESTING AND STORAGE

The fresh leaves and stalks can be harvested as needed. If used for wreaths or crafts, they will dry in place.

USES

Used for crafts and as an ornamental in the garden. Can be used as hedges, edgings, borders or ground covers or in rock gardens. Use in wreaths and other crafts.

GINGER

Zingiber officinale
Tender Perennial (culinary, medicinal)
Zone 9-10

HISTORY

Ginger's generic name, *zingiber,* is from the Sanskrit word, *shringavera,* which means "shaped like a deer's antlers." This is probably referring to the knobby look of the rhizome. It is uncertain whether ginger originated in ancient China or India, but 4400 years ago, bakers in Greece were using China-imported ginger to make gingerbread. This is one of the oldest and most important spices; where it originated does not matter. An empire's measure of wealth and power was measured in its trading successes with spices. Spanish colonizers and conquistadors introduced ginger around the world and especially in Jamaica and promoted its cultivation. Even today, Jamaican ginger is considered some of the best.

The Egyptian slaves ate unleavened sweet ginger cakes while building the pyramids. In the Dark Ages it was grown in the monastery gardens and by the 13th century it was so valued it became a bartering item. A pound of ginger in England during the

Middle Ages sold for one-shilling-seven-pence, which was about the same as the price of buying a sheep. During this time, only the upper class and royalty could afford to use ginger.

Ginger prices must have come down by the time of the Revolutionary War. Ginger rations were handed out to the American soldiers as a part of their diet. New Englanders during this period commonly ate ginger jam to prevent belching and flatulence.

It is a custom for the Chinese to place candied ginger in beautiful porcelain jars and present it to guests after meals to aid in digestion.

DESCRIPTION

A tall perennial, ginger reaches 3 to 5 feet high. It spreads freely by forming a large, knobby rhizome underground. It is a stout, buff-colored, aromatic, tuberous rhizome with swollen finger-like joints. Long upward-reaching stems project from each knob to produce broad, bright green leaf blades. It rarely blooms in cultivation, but when it does the yellow or white flowers appear in spikes 3 to 4 inches long. Place the container in shade in a rich, well drained soil, preferably in a tropical-like climate.

The flavor produced by ginger seems to be half spice and half citrus with a warm aroma and hot and slightly biting taste. It has warming, aromatic properties. Traditionally a home remedy for colds and flu, ginger promotes sweating which helps to rid toxins from the body. It can be taken as a tea with honey and lemon when you first notice a chill. It certainly has a calming effect on the digestive system and it has been used for travel sickness.

PLANTING AND PROPAGATION

This is a tropical plant and is found growing wild in tropical rain forests. In most areas of the United States, it must be grown in containers so it can be easily brought in during the winter months. Buy fresh roots at the supermarket, cut into pieces if you want several plants or use the whole root. Sprouts will grow from the eyes on the rhizome, very similar to potato sprouts.

Plant early in the summer and locate in partial shade. Select a container that is at least 12 inches deep and fill with moist, rich soil with some added sand. Be sure to provide good drainage. Let the rhizome dry for a couple of days to help prevent root rot. Place the eyes just below the surface of the soil. Put the pot in a warm and sunny spot and to avoid root rot, water sparingly until growth develops. After green shoots appear, water well. Keep misted to maintain high humidity and set up a regular fertilizer program. Move the plants indoors in the winter. They will become dormant and will die down. Repot each spring to accommodate growth.

HARVESTING AND STORAGE

When the ginger plant is well established, in about one year, dig up roots from young sprouts. These are the most flavorful. Cut away as much root as you need and replant the remaining rhizome. Roots will keep in the refrigerator for several months. Wrap them first in a paper towel, then wrap tightly in plastic.

Ginger root will keep indefinitely in a jar covered with sherry. And the nice part of this is when you have used all the ginger from the sherry you have a flavored sherry to use in your stir-fry dishes. If you try drying the root, shave slices and dry. You can then grind into powder and store in jars. Ginger also freezes well if stored in a plastic storage bag.

USES

The part used is the rhizome. Fresh ginger can be used in recipes that call for dried, but use only about half the amount. For Oriental or stir-fry dishes, peel fresh ginger root and chop into thin slivers. Cook in hot olive oil with green onions until flavored, then add whatever vegetable, fish or meat you have chosen as the main ingredient and stir quickly until cooked. The Chinese use ginger to hide the strong animal tastes of meat and fish.

Cook ginger in curry dishes or try homemade gingerbread with a dollop of whipped cream. Add it to beverages, especially ginger tea. Add it to fruit salads, meats, poultry, preserves, pickles, sweet potatoes, squash, carrots, pumpkin, rhubarb and peaches. Cook it along with onions and garlic. Ground ginger improves sweet puddings, quick breads, muffins, cakes and cookies.

If you do not choose to grow ginger, it is available commercially - fresh, dried ground, dried pieces, or candied slivers. Slivers are a nice addition to fresh peaches and strawberries.

Travelers should carry candied ginger or ginger pills with them to treat travel sickness. Ginger beer is also very popular.

HOREHOUND

Marrubium vulgare
Hardy Perennial (culinary, medicinal, ornamental, tea)
Zones 4-8

HISTORY

The name horehound is a derivitive of Horus, the Egyptian god of sky and light. In the early history of Greece, horehound was used to treat mad dog bites. It was also believed horehound could break magic spells. It was believed to improve conditions of tumors, tuberculosis, typhoid, snakebite, worms, itches and bronchitis. In modern times, it's included in some cough syrups and candies to help alleviate sore throats.

DESCRIPTION

A member of the mint family, menthol-flavored and very easy to grow, horehound spreads quickly. A hardy, erect perennial that is native to southern Europe and North Africa, it has naturalized in North America. It can survive on as little as 12 inches of water a year and enjoys the sun and drought. It has crinkled, woolly, greenish white leaves covered with hairs and equally hairy stems with a height growth of about 2 feet. It produces tiny, white flowers during June through September of the second year.

PLANTING AND PROPAGATION

Horehound is a slow germinator, but grows strongly and easily from seed sown on poor and arid soil. To increase the length of life enrich the soil with moist compost or well-rotted manure. Sow the seed ⅛ inch

deep in early spring. Cuttings are also easy to root and divisions can be taken.

Plant seedlings 1 foot apart; divide every 3 to 4 years. Horehound benefits from a good pruning in the springtime.

HARVESTING AND STORAGE

Horehound does not produce flowers until the second season, but the plant can be cut for drying or for use during the first year. The stalks can be harvested soon after flowering occurs. Air dry in a shaded area to retain the best color. The leaves should be harvested and dried when the flowers appear, by placing on drying screens or paper. Once they are dry, store in air tight containers. Fresh use is the preferred method for using horehound.

USES

Tea can be prepared using the leaves, however, this plant is used mostly as an ornamental with its silvery gray appearance. Horehound is used in veterinary practice for some horse ailments. It is used in flavoring candy, tea and coughdrops. Dried branches are used in floral arrangements.

HORSERADISH

Armoracia rusticana
Perennial (cosmetic, culinary, medicinal)
Zones 5-8

HISTORY

Originating on the borders of Europe and Asia, the horseradish was common to the table of only the Germans and the Danes until the end of the Middle Ages. It was accepted by everyone else, until then, as only a medicine.

The horseradish was considered a digestive aid in the early history of the Greeks. It was used as a cure for scurvy, since it contains high amounts of Vitamin C. It was also used cosmetically to fade freckles.

DESCRIPTION

This plant is a hardy perennial and a member of the mustard family. It is an invasive plant and if kept in an area to itself, can be allowed to grow wild. Grown for its deep taproot, it sprouts a group of large, coarse, yellow-green, glossy leaves. It rises to a height of 2 to 3 feet and spreads to 18 inches. If the weather is just right, it will form small white flowers atop a single spike in the summer. Its root has a very sharp, biting, pungent flavor much like a hot radish.

PLANTING AND PROPAGATION

Root cuttings are the usual means of propagation since seeds do not reproduce well. The roots can be purchased at your local grocer. In the spring, cuttings should be planted in rows spacing 15 to 18 inches apart. Plant in a well-drained, fertile and sunny area. Keep watered and well-weeded during hot spells.

HARVESTING AND STORAGE

By late fall the roots can be dug, since they grow fastest during late summer and early fall. Except in severe winter areas, the roots can be left in the ground and dug as needed, if well mulched. If kept harvest-

ed each year, this plant should not become too much of a pest.

USES

One of the best methods of grating the root is to peel the plant, preferably with rubber gloves on your hands. Cut into thin slices and place in a blender or food processor and grate with a small amount of vinegar. Let it sit covered for half an hour or so and then place in small, covered jars to store in the refrigerator. The mixture will keep for about three months if kept refrigerated.

Serve with most meats, especially beef. A good sauce is to blend equal parts of sour cream with the horseradish and you will have a tasty condiment for your entreé. A tasty sauce for seafood is made by mixing together lemon juice, grated horseradish root and catsup.

HYSSOP

Hyssopus officinalis
Hardy perennial (cosmetic, crafts, medicinal, ornamental)
Zones 3-9

HISTORY

Hyssop's name is derived from the Hebrew word *azob,* meaning "holy plant." It was used for purifying the temples. One of the earliest references to hyssop was in the 7th century, describing it as a strewing herb in sick rooms. Every monastery garden included hyssop to ward off the evil eye and to purge skin spots.

The Elizabethans used hyssop in their knot gardens and kept it in their sick rooms to cure coughs, rheumatism, toothaches and ringing ears. They also believed it to kill head lice.

DESCRIPTION

Hyssop, with its square stem, is a member of the mint family. It grows wild throughout the United States, but originated in the Middle East, eventually appearing in Europe and Asia. It is a hardy evergreen and can be harvested all year. The leaves are narrow, dark green and shiny with tiny blue flowers blooming from late summer to mid-fall. Hyssop grows from 18 to 30 inches high and spreads to 12 inches, maintaining a tidy shape. The blue flowers attract honeybees, hummingbirds and butterflies.

PLANTING AND PROPAGATION

Plant hyssop in a light well-drained high-lime soil in full sun or partial shade. Sow seed ¼ inch deep in early spring, thinning plants to 1 foot apart after seedlings appear. Hyssop will grow to about 1 to 2 feet tall but prune back to 6 inches in the spring and replenish the soil with compost. Replace the plants every 4 or 5 years. Cuttings or divisions can be made in spring or fall.

Flowers appear in June and will continue into August if conditions are right. The colors range from blue, violet, and to pink.

HARVESTING AND STORAGE

To retain the flower's deep blue color, cut flowering stalks just after the buds open. Air-dry them by hanging upside down in a warm, dark place.

USES

Use hyssop externally as a poultice for black eyes and bruising. Hyssop is used for a soothing bath mixed with rosemary, thyme, and mint. It makes an excellent border plant in knot gardens and attacts honeybees, hummingbirds, and butterflies. Use it in most crafts, such as soaps, perfumes, potpourris, wreaths, floral arrangements and in facials.

LAMB'S EARS

Stachys byzantina
Hardy perennial (dye, medicinal, ornamental)
Zones 4-8

HISTORY

Lamb's ears have long been used for Victorian tussie-mussies, nosegays with symbolic meaning. In the language of flowers, lamb's ears symbolize support, softness, gentleness and surprise. This is well earned. To touch one of the petals of this plant is to experience a softness and gentleness not found elsewhere. Childen of all ages love to stroke the leaves.

Lamb's ears were once used to soothe cuts which occurred when shearing wool from lambs. They were once used as a wound covering and poultice.

DESCRIPTION

Lamb's ears is a low-growing perennial which is winter hardy throughout most of the South. It produces 4-to-6-inch pointed, fuzzy, silvery-gray leaves which form a thick mat. The leaves prevent weeds from growing up around the plant. Late in the spring 12 to 18 inch stalks appear with pink or purple flowers. If the stalks bother you, simply snip off or plant the Silver Carpet variety which does not flower.

In winter, the fuzzy leaves insulate the plant while providing a silvery green touch to your garden.

PLANTING AND PROPAGATION

This is probably one of the easiest herbs to grow. Plant in full sun and any well-drained soil. It does not like to sit in wet areas. After heavy rains, to keep the plant looking neat, pull out the matted leaves at the bottom of the plant. It performs better in dry climates.

Sowing seed in early spring for the flowering types will produce flowers the next season.

It grows to a height of 4 to 15 inches, and should be planted 12 inches apart. If you would like large leaves, plant in a richer soil. Divisions can be made in early spring or autumn. Self-sown transplants will appear all around the plant, which can then be moved. It is also spread by stems that tunnel below the ground or grow across the top of it. These can be easily controlled by pulling out.

HARVESTING AND STORAGE

Stalks can be harvested as they bloom for use in flower arrangements. The leaves should be picked in clusters while they are soft and dried face down on screens, or if picked with stems intact, suspended through a screen.

USES

Use in tussie-mussies and for making wreaths. For dye makers, this herb yields a yellow dye. Flowers are beautiful in arrangements.

LAVENDER

Lavandula
Perennial (cosmetic, culinary, medicinal, ornamental)
Zones 5-9

HISTORY

Lavender is native to the Mediterranean region and has become naturalized in the southern climates of America. It grows wild in southern France, Spain and Italy. It is widely cultivated commercially, especially in France and Great Britain. The name comes from the Latin word *lavare* meaning "to wash." Lavender was widely used to scent baths and washing waters for clothing and as a strewing herb.

Cultivation of lavender began in England the 16th century and it was brought to America by the Pilgrims. The Victorians are closely associated with lavender. They used lavender to scent their gardens, their parlors and boudoirs. Linens were packed with sachets of lavender pressed between layers. They created fans to refresh themselves in the summer heat. Soaps and lotions were scented with lavender.

Lavender was used as a sedative and to help with hysteria. Even today, herbalists recommend the flowers or the oil for tension and nervous headaches. It is effective for healing burns and scalds. It is an insect repellent and, therefore, useful in the storage of linens.

DESCRIPTION

Lavender is a member of the mint family, growing to about 3 feet high and aproximately 2 feet wide. Tiny lavender flowers, which have a very refreshing smell, appear on fragrant, short, woody, spiky stems. The leaves are narrow and linear and form a spike of 5 to 7 whorls, putting forth a scent of mixed spice and a little touch of turpentine. The plant is bushy with leaves of gray-green to silver-gray covered with tiny white hairs. The blooming period is from mid-summer to early autumn, with the spikey flowers scenting the entire garden. After flowering, trim back hard to keep the growth compact and bushy.

Some varieties include Hidcote, which is a neat and compact form with deep purple flowers. Alba has white flowers and adapts well to most situations, growing to about 4 feet and hardy to 0°F. English lavender, (*Lavandula angustifolia)* is very dependable and aromatic, but suffers during hot, humid weather. Munstead is a dwarf, reaching 18 inches high with deep, lavender flowers. It blooms a little earlier than most varieties. French lavender, (*Lavandula dentata*) is only hardy to 15°F. It will grow up to 36 inches high with dark, lavender flowers in short clusters.

Depending on the variety and weather conditions, lavender often keeps its foliage and fragrance during the winters.

PLANTING AND PROPAGATION
Purchase transplants from a reliable

nursery and plant 24 inches apart and 6 inches deep in a sunny location. Plant in soil that drains well and does not contain a lot of clay. Clay soil will retain water and cause root rot and certain death for your plants. Lavender is usually drought tolerant. Deadhead during the summer to promote new flowering.

Divisions, layering or cuttings are ways to increase the number of lavender plants in your garden. For cuttings, take 2-to-3-inch long cuttings from side shoots. Do not cut from the mother plant. Simply rip a shoot downward getting a piece of the older wood with it. Set in a moist, sandy soil. Cover the roots and water in to fill in any air pockets. Keep the soil moist, not soggy, during the first season or until it is well developed. Add fertilizer soon after planting and again the next spring. A dash of lime will help its growth also. Plants will probably need replacing after 5 years.

HARVESTING AND STORAGE

When drying, to prevent flowers from falling off the stem, snip when the flowers are in bud stage. Strip the lower leaves from the stems and gather the lavender into a bundle consisting of several stems. Fasten with a rubber band and hang upside down in a warm dry place, preferably with little light so as to retain the color. Pick the stems in midday when the oils are most concentrated and the dew is dry. The flowers should be showing some color, but not in full bloom. The seeds can be harvested when mature. They are also very aromatic.

USES

Lavender is a wonderful herb to work with in the garden and it's quite useful and fun to find new uses. The flowers, seeds and oil are used.

Flowers can be crystallized for cake decorations or you can toss a sprig of its blossoms into a footbath and feel how it quickly revives tired feet. Go a little further and put several sprigs in the bathwater and your whole body will feel invigorated.

Use lavender leaves to flavor jellies, sugars and vinegars. Use flowers and leaves in potpourri or in sachets to tuck among linens and clothes in drawers and closets. Use leaves and flowers to perfume soaps and bath powders. Make wreaths and floral arrangements with fresh flowers.

Strip flowers from the stems and tie in a bundle for use while grilling. Soak for 20 to 30 minutes prior to tossing onto the hot coals. Use the stems for skewers. The stems will also serve as firelighters.

LEMON BALM
Melissa officinalis
Perennial (aromatic, cosmetic, culinary, medicinal)
Zones 4-9

HISTORY

Lemon balm attracts bees and thus its name, *melissa*, the Greek word for bee. In times past, the crushed leaves were applied to wounds to fight infection. It is said to have a calming effect, much like valium. Drinks were concocted using lemon balm for the cure of headaches. Arabs believed

lemon balm was good for heart disorders and lifting of the spirits.

Laboratory studies show lemon balm does have a sedative effect on the central nervous system of mice. It also seems to prevent the spread of bacteria and viruses.

Beekeepers rub the inside of hives with lemon balm to encourage bees to remain and orchard growers plant lemon balm near fruit trees to encourage bees and promote pollination to their trees.

DESCRIPTION

Lemon balm is a member of the mint family and has a four-sided stem as mints do. It grows to approximately 2 to 3 feet tall with aromatic, toothed, bright green, heart-shaped leaves. It gives off a strong scent of lemon when crushed. Producing small whitish flowers in mid-summer, the plant is thick and bushy, dying back in the fall but appearing again in early spring.

PLANTING AND PROPAGATION

Lemon balm is grown easily from seed and germinates best if the seeds are not covered. You can propagate by layering or by division in spring. Cuttings can also be taken. Plant in a well-drained, sun-lit soil; it will tolerate some shade. Lemon balm will self-sow and spread by roots, so allow plenty of room. It is not an invasive plant like its relative, mint. To keep the plant bushy, simply keep it pinched back.

HARVESTING AND STORAGE

Harvest prior to flowering for the most flavorful and aromatic leaves. To harvest, clip leaves off as needs arise, or in spring, cut off the entire plant 2 inches above the ground, being careful not to bruise the leaves. Lemon balm should be dried very quickly. If the entire plant is cut in the spring, another crop should appear by summer. If you want to use the leaves in a potpourri, gather the lower leaves late in the summer. The lower leaves are richest in essential oil. For those times when only fresh will do, freezing maintains a freshness acceptable for cooking.

USES

Lemon balm has a special effect on wood. When it is rubbed in, it leaves a lustrous shine and a wonderful aroma. Try it on your furniture. It is still the oil used in lemon oil furniture polish today.

Lemon balm is also nice added to cookies, teas and cakes. Its leaves are used to flavor poultry, fish dishes and salads. Jellies and jams seem to have an added zest with lemon balm added.

Potpourri benefits from the use of the leaves of lemon balm with their strong, lemony scent. The leaves are a nice addition to herb bath mixtures and, used as a steamy facial, gives relief from acne.

LEMONGRASS

Cymbopogon citratus
Tender Perennial (cosmetic, culinary, tea)
Zones 9-10

HISTORY

Tropical Southeast Asia is home to the aromatic lemongrass, fast becoming one of the most important lemon flavorings used

in a number of cuisines, especially in Thai cooking. It is being grown commercially in Florida for use by confectioners in making artificially flavored lemon candy.

DESCRIPTION

Lemongrass, a member of the grass family, has a long, thin, light green stalk, much like a green onion. It is a semi-tropical, grass-like herb with billowing blades and reaching 2 to 4 feet tall. Use for a beautiful vertical accent plant in your garden to serve as an ornamental grass. This plant has a distinct lemon flavor with a hint of ginger.

In cold winter areas, it should be brought indoors or placed in a cold frame or greenhouse.

Lemongrass is also known as "fever grass" and used to treat fevers.

PLANTING AND PROPAGATION

Lemongrass is an easy to grow plant if begun with transplants or divisions. It requires full sun and average, well-drained sandy soil. Apply a slow-release fertilizer before or during planting and again in the spring. Take care not to overwater. If the plant is too large to take inside, plant a division and keep it indoors to set out in the spring. Before dividing, prune the plant to several
inches.

HARVESTING AND STORAGE

Cut fresh foliage as needed anytime in the summer. Cut the foliage back to within 3 inches of the ground in the fall. Dry quickly for best flavor by hanging cut pieces in a cool, dry place or on a screen in a cool oven (warm setting with the door open) or freeze. Lemon balm or lemon peel can be a good substitute.

USES

To use, discard the rough outer leaves and about 2 to 3 inches of the thick root end. This will leave the tender stalk, which can be sliced or chopped.

Lemongrass makes a wonderful lemon tea, using dried herb, crumbled and mixed with mint, rosemary and chamomile.

Use it in stir fry foods, poultry, seafood.

It can also be used as a hair rinse.

LOVAGE

Levisticum officinale
Hardy Perennial (culinary, medicinal)
Zones 5-8

HISTORY

During the Middle Ages, lovage was popular for its culinary as well as its medicinal importance. Early herbalists used lovage roots as a diuretic and in treating kidney stones. Even now, some Europeans use it as a folk cure for minor stomachaches and headaches.

In the 17th century the British herbalist, Culpeper, recommended "half a dram of the powdered root, taken in wine," to "warm a cold stomach, help digestion, and consume all raw and superfluous moisture therein." It was used as a bath herb and even called a love potion.

DESCRIPTION

Lovage has been described as a "giant version of celery," sometimes called smallage. And, indeed, it can be used as a substitute for celery. All of its parts are useful in cooking and with its bright, shiny foliage, it makes a good background plant in your garden. It is native to the Balkans and the Mediterranean area.

Lovage can grow to 6 to 7 feet high and 18 inches wide. Small, yellow flowers appear in early spring. It has a beautiful bronze color while very young. Each year in the winter, it will die down to the ground only to appear again in the spring.

PLANTING AND PROPAGATION

Lovage is partial to full sun with a little shade and fertile, moist, well-drained soil. If sowing seed, sow thickly since it tends to have a poor germination. Sow shallowly in late summer or early fall. After the seedlings appear, thin to 2 to 3 feet apart. During the flowering period, June to July, prune away flowers to encourage the growth of its foliage. Its flowers, which appear on umbels, and are tiny and greenish-yellow, will reseed vigorously if left on the plant.

Lovage can grow to a height of 6 feet with hollow, ribbed stems and glossy dark green leaves. The roots can be divided, but be sure to have a strong bud on each division and set 2 feet apart. The plant will be bigger and stronger. Each spring, replenish the soil with manure or compost.

HARVESTING AND STORAGE

Once lovage is established, the leaves can be harvested for fresh use. Seeds are ready for harvesting once the fruits are brown and begin to pop open. The roots can be dug in late fall but wait until the plant is 2 years old. Wash and slice the root into ½-inch pieces and dry before storing. Branches can be bundled together and hung to dry. For the best flavor, cut the stems just prior to the flower's setting seed.

USES

Often compared to celery or parsley, use the leaves fresh to flavor salads, soups, stews, vegetables, meats, poultry, sauces, or even in *bouquet garni*. The stems can be blanched and eaten as a vegetable or candied. Sprinkle lovage seed over meat, bread or cookies. Lovage works well with potatoes, especially potato salad, tomatoes, chicken, poultry stuffings and vegetables. If you plan on using lovage in your soups and stews, simply chop the blanched herb and freeze it in ice cube trays. If you prefer drying, bunch together and hang it upside down. Store it in a tightly sealed opaque container.

MARJORAM

Origanum majorana
Tender perennial (aromatic, culinary, medicinal, ornamental)
Zones 6-10

HISTORY

The Greeks used marjoram to cure rheumatism and claimed marjoram was precious to Aphrodite, the goddess of love. This gave rise to the custom of making garlands from marjoram for weddings. The marjoram, sometimes called knotted marjoram and

a member of the mint family, is sweet marjoram. There are several marjorams and while oregano and marjoram are sometimes confused, marjoram has the milder taste, while oregano is stronger and sharper.

DESCRIPTION

Sweet marjoram (*M. hortensis*), valued for its kitchen use, is usually grown as an annual, since it has a shallow root system and a bushy growth. Its square stems and grayish leaves are covered with small hairs. Growing to a height of about 1 foot and flowering in late summer with tiny white or pink flowers, marjoram is one of the pleasures of herb gardening. Its taste has a sweet, spicy flavor with a minty aftertaste.

PLANTING AND PROPAGATION

Plant in full sun in a light, dry, well-drained soil. The seeds will germinate quickly, but the seedlings are weak and subject to damping off. In March, sow seeds in pots located in a sunny location inside. Transplant to the garden after all danger of frost is past. Stem cuttings and root division are also used to propagate marjoram. To encourage bushy growth, pinch back before flowering. In order to avoid confusion with oregano, plant marjoram with your annuals.

HARVESTING AND STORAGE

Begin harvesting fresh leaves about 6 weeks after transplanting. Hang upside down for drying and strip the leaves from the stem for storage when drying is complete. Marjoram retains its flavor after drying but sweet marjoram leaves do not freeze well. It can be potted up and brought into the house for use in cooking during the winter.

USES

Folk remedies for this herb include treatments for asthma, toothaches, and rheumatism. Marjoram is used in bathing, in potpourri and in sachets.

Its culinary use is the greatest. Add chopped leaves to salads; use with most meats, fish, poultry, vegetables, and Italian foods. Use it to flavor vinegars, soups and stuffings. Sprinkle a few leaves over a fruit salad. Add some leaves in a saucer of oil for a delicious bread dip. It is one of the herbs used in *bouquet garni* and serves as a substitute for oregano in most cases; just use twice as much. Marjoram is used in bathing, in potpourri, and in sachets.

MINT

Mentha
Perennial (aromatic, culinary, medicinal, ornamental)
Zones 5-9

HISTORY

Mint originated in Europe but in India it hangs in windows and doorways to scent rooms. In Greece, it is rubbed on a table to freshen it before being set for guests. It is a very refreshing herb and one of the most popular and well-known. It offers cool and refreshing relief in the summer.

Named after Menthé, a mythological Greek goddess, whose punishment by a vengeful and jealous wife was to be cast onto the ground and trampled upon forever.

Pluto, smitten by the goddess, tried unsuccessfully to undo the spell created by his wife but did make Menthé into a wonderfully fragrant plant to be walked upon.

DESCRIPTION

Mints have square stems, making them very distinctive, and with opposite-paired leaves very easy to spot. Most of the mints are very invasive, spreading prolifically by their root system on runners. These upright perennials grow to 3 feet tall, with tiny white to purplish blooms appearing on spikes at the tips of the stems and blooming from mid to late summer.

Growing mint for its wonderful aroma is reason enough to plant it. Pinch a leaf off and take a whiff as you walk by. Take a breath of air into your mouth as you chew on a leaf. It's wonderfully refreshing!

There are an infinite number of varieties of mint and mints cross-breed so easily, sometimes making it hard to identify the plant. Some of the well-known varieties are pennyroyal, peppermint, apple or wooly mint, spearmint (preferred by cooks), and Corsican mint.

PLANTING AND PROPAGATION

It would be advice well taken if you plant mint in a container which will prevent the plant from spreading. One idea is a tub or bottomless pail sunk into the ground. Another would be a separate garden entirely, where you can contain the roots, or even in a window box. A clay pot will crack under pressure from the root system and roots will creep out of any pot with a drainage hole in the bottom. I planted mint, after experiencing its tenacity, in an unused sandbox. It seems to thrive in the mix of sand and soil.

Mint prefers full sun to partial shade and thrives in areas with plenty of moisture. Since seeds may not grow true, begin with plants from a nursery, setting out in the early spring. After that, cuttings of runners can be transplanted very easily.

Renew beds every 3 to 4 years in the fall by pulling up roots, dividing and replanting. Its major enemy is rust disease appearing on the leaves. If this should occur, destroy the bed and begin again.

HARVESTING AND STORAGE

Harvesting leaves of mint can begin in early spring through late fall. In fact, harvesting sprigs will keep the plant neat and trim. Harvest just before flowering for the most flavorful leaves. Just clip off bunches and hang to dry, or use fresh. Mint freezes well, so bag some up for use in the winter. However, fresh mint is always best.

During the summer, pinch the tops out to prevent flowering. At the end of summer, cut back the plant to the ground. This will prevent pests from using the plant as a winter "hide-away." Cut mints to the ground in the middle of summer and you will reap a second crop a few weeks later.

USES

Of course, when mint is mentioned, the first thing coming to mind is mint julep, a famous southern drink. But mint, especially spearmint, is good for flavoring sauces, iced drinks-especially tea, and works well with jams and jellies. Mint is traditionally served with lamb dishes, dishes with peas and

potatoes and commonly used as a garnish. Dip the leaves in lightly beaten egg whites, then in sugar and dry on waxed paper for crystallized mint.

Try mint in potpourri or sachets. As a cure for headache, take fresh peppermint leaves, crush them and apply to the forehead. This is great for aching muscles, too. Mint is a breath freshener-simply chew on a few leaves and taste the refreshing, cool, minty feel it gives to your mouth.

NASTURTIUM

Tropaeolum majus
Annual (culinary, ornamental)
Zones 3-9

HISTORY

A South American native, the nasturtium found its way to Europe by way of Spanish conquistadors. By the late 1500s it had arrived in England and was then spread throughout Asia. Nasturtiums gained favor rapidly in kitchens and gardens. It was recognized as a beautiful flower for the gardens and a tasteful addition to cooking. Having spread to America, Thomas Jefferson kept this plant in his garden. At the time of his presidency, his nasturtium garden was a total of 190 square yards.

DESCRIPTION

The nasturtium is very easy to grow. There are many varieties - climbing, creeping and low growing - making them useful in most situations. They sport large round, bright green leaves which are dotted with open-faced flowers in various shades ranging from creamy white, yellow-orange, red, and maroon. Once they bloom, they bloom on into the fall.

PLANTING AND PROPAGATION

Seeds should be planted in March in most areas. Set the seeds about 1 foot apart in full sun in any ordinary soil with good drainage. First soak the seeds overnight in a small amount of water.
Germination will take about a week, leaves will appear in 10 days, and flowers in 10 to 12 weeks. Production of flowers depends on the soil - the poorer the soil, the more flowers; in a richer soil, more leaves will be produced.

HARVESTING AND STORAGE

The flowers, leaves and seed pods of nasturtiums are edible. The flavor is peppery, tangy and mustard-like. Harvest flowers just as they open, washing well before tossing into your salad.

USES

Add petals of nasturtiums to your salads for color and flavor. Add nasturtium to butters, cream cheese; use it to flavor oils, vinegars and dressings. Use as a garnish. The leaves are high in vitamin C and thought to relieve cold symptoms.

OREGANO

Origanum
Perennial (aromatic, culinary, medicinal, ornamental)
Zones 5-9

HISTORY

Sometimes called wild marjoram, oregano is native to the Mediterranean part of Europe and has been enjoyed by the people in that area for centuries. The word oregano means "joy of the mountain" coming from the Greek *oros*, meaning "mountain," and *ganos*, meaning "joy." Used mostly for cooking, we recognize it quickly in Greek cuisine. It is widely used in Mexican and Italian foods, as a basic ingredient to pizza sauce, spaghetti sauce and many of the international spicy dishes using tomatoes.

Oregano contains antioxidants which research indicates may inhibit damage to cells that can lead to cancer.

DESCRIPTION

Like its relative marjoram, oregano is a member of the mint family and has the same characteristic square stems. It is an aromatic, herbaceous perennial which grows to a height of 1 to 3 feet with erect, hairy stems and purple-white flowers appearing in late summer. Oregano has leaves appearing opposite and has a bushy growth, however, unlike marjoram, you can treat oregano as a perennial. Its taste is very clove-like and slightly bitter, stronger than marjoram.

PLANTING AND PROPAGATION

This plant tolerates either full sun or partial shade in light, well-drained soil. In the spring, you can start plants inside in pots and transplant them to the garden when any danger of frost is past. Stem cuttings and root division are methods used successfully with oregano for propagation. Plant approximately 16 inches apart, giving them room for their bushy growth. For maintentance during the growing period, pinch to prevent flowering during the summer.

HARVESTING AND STORAGE

You can begin harvesting oregano just before the plant blooms, cutting above the lowest set of leaves. New leaves will soon appear, giving you more tender leaves to harvest later in the summer. Hang to dry, stripping leaves from stems when dry. Store in airtight containers.

Since fresh herbs are always best, be sure to freeze some, too. Store leaves in plastic storage bags, forcing excess air out and sealing tightly.

USES

This plant makes an attractive border in the garden, but clearly is best utilized in the kitchen. Use oregano in vinegars, salads, Mexican dishes, chili, Italian dishes, tomato dishes, meats, cheese, fish, eggs, snap beans and all mushroom dishes. When making vinegar, toss a few oregano blossoms into the jar.

Dried leaves are often added to potpourri. Use oregano in fresh flower arrangements to sweeten the air.

PARSLEY
Petroselinum crispum
Biennial (culinary, medicinal, ornamental)
Zones 5-9

HISTORY

Greeks fed parsley to their chariot horses to make them run faster and then crowned the winning horseman with wreaths made of parsley. They also used parsley in funeral ceremonies by sprinkling corpses with it to deoderize them.

In addition to its use as a garnish, parsley has a high content of chlorophyll, making it a wonderful breath freshener. The Romans set an example by using parsley to disguise the smell of alcohol on their breath. Parsley is one of the herbs in *fines herbes* along with chives, tarragon and chervil.

DESCRIPTION

Parsley is a hardy biennial, growing to 12 to 18 inches tall. It is a good source of vitamins A and C, iron, phosphorus, calcium, iron and manganese. With tiny yellow-green flowers appearing in early summer, this herb has a very orderly growing habit by forming a beautiful, graceful mound. The color can be yellowish-green to a dark green, depending on the soil. Producing foliage the first year and flowers the second, it is usually grown as an annual since the leaves lose most of their taste after flowering.

Three of the most common varieties are the flat-leaf (Italian), resembling coriander, the curly leaf, and Hamburg (the parsnip rooted). Curly parsley has a pepper-like taste and is widely used as a garnish, while the flat-leaf variety has a richer, more robust flavor and is preferred for cooking. The Hamburg variety has a taste much like celery and is grown for its root which can be used in soups or anywhere you need the flavor of celery.

PLANTING AND PROPAGATION

Parsley's reputation of being hard to germinate is well-earned. Seeds are the only way to propagate and they can take 6 to 8 weeks to germinate. You can speed this up by providing a little warmth, perhaps in a greenhouse or under a grow-light 6 to 8 weeks before the last frost in your area. Or you can soak the seeds for 24 hours in warm water and pour boiling water into prepared drills prior to planting.

Sow seeds in the garden after the soil warms in the spring and again in late summer. In the South, it is best to plant in the fall. Plant 6 to 8 inches apart in full sun or partial shade. Don't let parsley get so dry it wilts, since this will cause browning of the edges. Plants can be covered by a frame in the winter or brought inside in pots after a light frost or two has fallen on them. Leave the Hamburg variety in the ground until ready to use.

HARVESTING AND STORAGE

Harvest the fresh leaves as needed by picking from the outer leaves. Freezing is the preferred method of preserving parsley. Parsley is hard to dry. However, try wrapping it in a paper towel, placing it inside a brown paper sack, fastening and keeping in the refrigerator for about 2 weeks. The color and flavor will be retained using this method.

USES

Of course, we all recognize parsley as a garnish. It's served on our plates at most restaurants. But, remember parsley is an odor eater, too. Remove fish taste and odor from hot oil simply by dropping a sprig or two into the oil. Rubbing parsley over your hands after cutting onions removes the smell.

Munch on the sprig of parsley served on your plate for garnish. It will freshen and sweeten your breath to hide the fact you have been eating onions or garlic. Plant near asparagus and it will work as an insect repellent against asparagus beetles.

Its greatest use is culinary. You can perk up most foods, with the possible exception of sweets, with parsley. Add near the end, or sprinkle on after cooking. Deep fry parsley and serve with fried foods. See how fast it disappears!

ROSEMARY

Rosemarinus officinalis
Tender Perennial (cosmetic, culinary, medicinal, ornamental)
Zones 7-10

HISTORY

Rosemary means "dew of the sea" and comes from the Latin *ros marinus*. Going back to the days of Christ's childhood, it's said the sky-blue color of the flower is a result of Mary drying her cloak on a rosemary bush. The Shakespearean play, Hamlet, referred to rosemary as a symbol of remembrance and fidelity. An English legend says, "Where rosemary flourisheth, the women ruleth."

Rosemary is believed to preserve youth. Even smelling rosemary was said to "keep thee youngly." It was worn at weddings as a symbol of fidelity, love and friendship and placed in courtrooms in bouquets, to offer protection against jail fever. It was commonly burned as incense in hospitals to prevent the spread of disease.

Rosemary contains antioxidants which may help to prevent cancer and is used by some to help ease indigestion.

DESCRIPTION

Rosemary is a bushy, perennial, evergreen shrub. It is a relative of lavender and a member of the mint family, with gray-green leaves very much resembling needles. The plant gives off a wonderful, sweet fragrance much like pine needles lying in the warm sun. Both flowers and oil are highly prized in the cosmetic industry for perfumes and toiletries.

Shrubs can grow from 3 to 5 feet tall in the garden. If grown as a houseplant, it will probably be no more than a foot high. It has square, brown, woody stems. Its leaves are narrow and pointed with pale blue, hooded flowers appearing from mid spring to early summer.

Depending on the variety, rosemary can serve many situations. The prostrate form is wonderful used in hanging baskets or draped over a rock wall. Prostrate rosemary can easily be trained into bonsai, while others can be cut into topiaries. Some have a spreading character and extend to eight feet, making a good ground cover. Since harsh winters are not hospitable to rosemary,

weather must be considered if used as a ground cover. For cooking, common rosemary (*R. officinalis*) is preferred. It is an upright shrub and hardy to 15°F.

For over-wintering outdoors, rosemary can be protected in the garden with a heavy mulch around the roots and a clear plastic tent covering. The tent should not touch the plant. Be sure to provide an escape route for the heat that gathers on a warm day. Simply snip holes in the sides or leave an opening at the bottom. Rosemary blooms well all winter under these conditions. If you have a greenhouse or cold frame, rosemary can be sheltered there safely.

For over-wintering indoors, bring your potted rosemary to a sunny location. Keep the spiney leaves misted and provide the plant with well-drained soil. Do not let the soil become soggy.

PLANTING AND PROPAGATION

It is difficult to grow rosemary from seed, so purchasing plants at a nursery is your best bet. Cuttings or divisions can also be made. Container gardening is a good alternative for rosemary since in most areas it must be brought inside when winter nears. Since rosemary likes warmth, plant in a sandy, well-drained soil in a sunny, sheltered location near a wall or in a corner. Plant it where you want it to remain since it does not transplant well. The oils are more fragrant if grown in poor soil. The plant will not tolerate wet roots. It does appreciate extra lime applied to its surrounding soil several times during the season. When watering, consider the fact that the leaves require moisture as well as the roots.

HARVESTING AND STORAGE

Harvest anytime during the year. To dry rosemary, simply hang branches until they are dry. You can easily strip the leaves from the branch. Or, freeze by putting them in plastic storage bags.

USES

Rosemary is commonly used with lamb and pork, but is good in cooking any meat, fish or poultry. Toss a few sprigs onto your hot coals when grilling pork for a subtle, pleasing flavor.

When dry, the leaves are sharp and spiky so they should either be crushed before using or a whole sprig placed in your cooking dish and later removed. Use rosemary enclosed in a cheesecloth bag for soups. It is wonderful used in herbal butters, jams and jellies, breads, vinegars and oils. Most vegetables are enhanced using rosemary. Use it in spinach, squash, peas, lentils, eggs, cheese and it works well with other herbs such as chives, thyme, chervil, parsley and bay. Bouquet garnis benefit from rosemary, as do stuffings. Add rosemary to apples and fruit drinks. Make rosemary vinegar and leave a fresh stem in the jar.

Cosmetically, dark hair will be enhanced by the use of a rosemary rinse. A bathbag added to your bathwater will act as an astringent to oily skin and you will find it very refreshing and stimulating.

SAGE

Salvia officinalis
Perennial (aromatic, cosmetic, culinary, medicinal, ornamental)
Zones 4-8

HISTORY

Greeks believed it to be the perfect flavoring. In the Middle Ages, there was a saying associating sage with longevity, "Why should a man die when there is sage in his garden?" Considered for centuries as an aid to increased mental capacity and a cure-all for ills, some types are beneficial for use in treating eye diseases, used as an expectorant, as an astringent and for a gargle.

DESCRIPTION

The Latin word *salvere* means "to save" and probably refers to its healing properties. Sage is a member of the mint family and a fast-spreading, evergreen shrub, growing about 2 feet tall. It has gray-green, fuzzy leaves, which are pebbly and decorative, with purple flowers appearing on spikes in summer. New plants will put forth flowers in their second summer. There are over 600 different varieties of sage. Several have multicolored leaves with one being tri-color, flashing leaves of pink, cream, and green. Most sages are a beautiful addition to any garden, be it herb or flower garden.

S. officinalis is the one we all expect to be flavoring the Thanksgiving turkey dressing.

PLANTING AND PROPAGATION

Sow seeds, where possible, in spring after danger of frost. Plants from the nursery take hold quickly, producing leaves for use. Cuttings taken in spring or late summer take root easily or try layering by pegging down stems until roots are present. Plant in a well-drained soil in a sunny location. Sage does not like for its roots to stay wet.

By pruning regularly, you can shape the bush. Prune back early in the spring to promote bushiness and immediately after the flowering period, also.

HARVESTING AND STORAGE

Harvest sage lightly the first year; after that, pick leaves as needed. Just before flowering is the best time for flavor. Flowering usually occurs in June and July. Cut the upper one-third of the plant in midsummer and again in the fall. If drying for future use, dry slowly and crumble to a fluffy powder which is called rubbed sage.

USES

Sage is traditionally used with fatty meats and in stuffings, along with onions, and as a spice in sausage. Sage is very versatile and does not lose its taste with cooking for long periods. Use it with pork, duck, cheese and tomato dishes. Add sage to cooked vegetables and fish. Fry the leaves of clary sage like fritters. Add some to the skillet when frying chicken.

Sage tea can be used as a rinse for dark hair, to help alleviate cold symptoms and to relieve headaches. Pineapple sage (a tender annual) can be added to potpourri, sachets and jams and jellies.

Deodorize a room by burning a sage leaf. Use leaves from a sage plant as a tooth-

brush to whiten your teeth and strengthen your gums. Sage is popularly used in wreath-making for its fragrance and beauty.

SALAD BURNET

Poterium Sanguisorba
Perennial (cosmetic, culinary, medicinal, ornamental)
Zones 5-10

HISTORY

Originating in the Mediterranean areas, salad burnet spread across Europe and became basically a fodder plant. Sir Francis Bacon said it should be walked on in paths to release the scent along with mints. Medicinally, it has been used for skin irritations and gout and fresh leaves have been used as an aid to indigestion. *Sanguisorba* means "drink up blood" and herbalists mixed a salad burnet tea to stop hemorrhages and as an ointment for wounds.

A note found in Thomas Jefferson's letters indicated he once sent a pair of lads to pick up 6 to 8 bushels of burnet seed. He was using burnet in his immense fields for fodder and erosion control, which was a common practice in colonial times.

DESCRIPTION

You can tell, with a glance at its leaves, that this plant is a member of the rose family. Its leaves are rounded and toothed, very similar to the rose. This may be the only member of the rose family to be considered an herb. It forms a beautiful rosette with dense leaves that may grow as high as a foot. Tall globe-like green flowers with red styles appearing in mid-summer are borne on a stem which may get as tall as 3 feet. However, the flowers don't appear until its second year.

PLANTING AND PROPAGATION

This plant can be easily grown by seeds. It self-sows freely and the resulting plants are usually stronger than the original. Root division in the spring is a good way to multiply your plants. You can also plant the mature seedhead. Plant in a well-drained soil. It benefits from lime and loves the open sunshine.

HARVESTING AND STORAGE

Burnet leaves do not dry well; they are best used fresh or frozen. Leaves can be preserved in vinegar without loss of color.

USES

Its taste is very much like cucumber and, when used in a salad, can serve as a substitute without the gastric after-effect of cucumbers. The use of salad burnet in cooking is limited since the leaves lose most of their flavor. Use salad burnet in wine cups or mixed into cream cheese and herbal butters, as well as a garnish.

Burnet is beautiful as a border plant since it remains useable until after the snows fall.

SAVORY

Satureja
Annual and perennial (culinary, medicinal, ornamental)
Zones 6-9

HISTORY

It's believed the Romans brought savory to England, where it became popular as a flavoring and in medicine. The name "savory" was applicable due to its spicy, peppery taste. It became the spice to use before the introduction of pepper.

Savory has a reputation for regulating the sex drive. However, summer and winter savories have different influences. Winter was thought to decrease the sexual drive and summer to increase the sexual appetites. Perhaps this is the reason summer savory is the one people prefer!

DESCRIPTION

Both the summer (*S. hortensis*) and winter (*S. montana*) varieties have peppery tastes, with summer's being just a little milder than winter's and more suited to culinary use. Known as the "bean herb" and used to flavor most fresh and dried vegetables of this type, summer savory is the larger and sweeter plant with slightly bronze, slender leaves and whitish to pinkish flowers. In most areas, winter savory is an evergreen with shiny, dark-green, pointed leaves and white or lavender flowers. For ornamental use in your garden, the winter variety is more suited as a landscape plant.

Summer savory grows to about 18 inches in height, while the winter savory grows to about 1 foot.

PLANTING AND PROPAGATION

Plant the summer annual in a rich soil where it will receive plenty of sun and some moisture. If planted in patches, it adds a nice ornamental touch to your garden, especially since it blooms from July to October. Plant seeds only about ⅛-inch deep.

The winter variety can withstand a poorer soil and less moisture. It is highly prized for its use as a border plant in knot gardens. Division or cuttings are an easy means of increase for this plant. Layering in the fall will also yield a nice plant to detach in the spring.

In the spring, cut the winter savory back severely to give it a fresh start. This variety should be replaced every three years to keep a good, healthy planting.

HARVESTING AND STORAGE

Begin harvesting before the plant flowers, for fresh or dried uses. Most of the flavor of savory is retained in the drying process. Freezing is also a good method of preserving the fresh flavor.

Winter savory can also be harvested lightly throughout the winter.

USES

Add savory to three-bean salad, all green salads and vegetables, especially fresh green beans. Some people plant savory near the green beans in their gardens so it can easily be picked along with the beans. Use in stuffings, sausages, cheese dishes, eggs, meat and fish; use anywhere you want a spicy, pep-

pery flavor. Use with cabbage, onions, peas, eggplant. Since it is claimed savory is an antiflatulent, add it to your dried beans while cooking.

The winter variety is a little stronger in flavor than the summer variety.

Both of these plants grow well in containers, pots and window boxes. However, if the winter variety is in a container, it must be brought in during the cold months.

SCENTED GERANIUM

Pelargonium
Tender Perennial (aromatic, culinary, ornamental)
Perennial in Zone 10, annual in cooler zones

HISTORY

Scented geranium is native to the Cape of Good Hope in South Africa and remained virtually unknown until 1847 when the French perfume industry realized and embraced its aromatic qualities. The herb was brought to America by the colonists. Thomas Jefferson is thought to have brought several varieties to the White House with him.

It was enjoyed by the Victorians, who brought scented geraniums inside their homes so their long skirts would rub against the leaves as they walked, thereby releasing their particular scent.

DESCRIPTION

If you grow scented geraniums in pots, let the roots become slightly cramped to encourage blooming. Height ranges 2 to 4 feet and 1 foot wide. Leaves are frilly or ruffled, velvety or smooth. Some are varigated. There is such a wide variety, they will continue to hold your interest. Some varieties lend themselves to hanging baskets or window boxes or any container, while some are a trailing variety and can be used as ground covers, or in flower borders.

There is the rose geranium (*Pelargonium graveolens*) which has a spicy, rose-scented foliage with small clusters of pink flowers. The leaves are dark green with tiny, white hairs. The apple-scented geranium (*P. odoratissimum*) is great for hanging baskets with its clusters of white flowers. The coconut-scented geraniu, (*P. grossularioides)* will work well in hanging baskets also. There are so many more scents: ginger, nutmeg, lemon, lime, licorice, strawberry.

The leaves store essential oils in tiny leaf cells called trichomes on the surface. At the slightest touch, their perfumes will be released and fill the air.

PLANTING AND PROPAGATION

Scented geranium enjoys full sun in cooler areas but needs partial shade in the hotter areas. It requires well-drained soil. If sowing seed, sow 2 months before last frost date because of the slow germination. In most areas, scented geraniums are grown as annuals since they are tender tropicals. Cuttings can be taken from new grown which root quickly and easily in the spring or fall. For winter blossoms indoors, take cuttings in the summer and place near a sunny window. When fertilizing, use very little or no nitrogen to get the best fragrance

from the plant. Take new cuttings from year-old plants and discard the old plant. Prune away dead foliage regularly.

HARVESTING AND STORAGE

Leaves can be harvested at any time during the season. The foliage and flowers are both edible. Dry the leaves by laying on a paper towel to dry. In the fall, prior to the first freeze, take off the top one-third of the plant and air-dry. Move the plant indoors for the winter since it is only hardy to about 20°F.

USES

The leaves and flowers of scented geranium are used for cooking and fragrances. Use in jellies, puddings, syrups, stuffings, punches, teas and vinegars. Use to flavor cakes or barbecue sauces, or fresh flowers for your salad. They are wonderful in herb butters.

The leaves are often used to make perfume and it is a sweet addition to sachets and potpourris. Add leaves to your bathwater. Infuse as a mild astringent to clean and help circulation of pale, sluggish complexions. It is commonly used in aromatherapy also.

Just a suggestion - but plant scented geraniums where you will rub against them just as the Victorians did.

SOAPWORT

Saponaria officinalis
Hardy Perennial (aromatic, cosmetic, medicinal, ornamental)
Zones 3-8

HISTORY

Romans used this handy herb to soften water. In the Middle Ages soapwort was grown in areas near wool mills. It was used to produce a soapy liquid to degrease and thicken woollen cloth. This method was known as "fulling." Soapwort's gentle cleaning action is ideal for tapestries and for delicate fabrics that would not survive washing in a product that is detergent-based. Museums today employ suds made from soapwort for laundering and revitalizing precious fabrics. The flower is sometimes used in brewing to produce a "head" on beer.

DESCRIPTION

A relative of pinks, soapwort will fill the air on hot summer evenings. It is sometimes called bouncing bet and wild sweet William. It is a native of western Asia and naturalized in the sunny waste places of eastern North America and Europe. It is common on roadsides, along railways, and on waste ground. It forms a dense tuft of ½-inch leaves that are nearly hidden by masses of small ¼-inch bright pink or white 5-petaled flowers which form in clusters.

Soapwort makes an excellent rock garden plant which blooms in early July and through September. It grows 1 to 2 feet tall, with a single, thick, slightly-branched stem with oval leaves which narrow to a point and

hug the stem. It contains saponins which lower the surface tension of water and produce a lather.

PLANTING AND PROPAGATION

Plant in full sun to light shade with well-drained average to poor soil. It will not tolerate soggy conditions. Plant seed in the spring or fall or sowing indoors in the late winter will produce earlier plants to transplant. After the plants are fully established, it will self-sow and spread rapidly. It can be propagated by division after becoming established. To maintain a compact form, trim back after flowering. It will bloom throughout much of the summer and early fall.

HARVESTING AND STORAGE

The roots and leaves can be harvested as needed. Clean, chop, and boil the root to make a sudsy solution. The juice from fresh leaves will relieve itching skin conditions. The roots contain the highest concentration of saponin, however, it is toxic.

USES

To make a mild soap or shampoo, soak and boil the dried root, or boil the fresh stems in rainwater for 30 minutes. This will yield a soapy sap. It sends forth a raspberry scent with just a hint of clove.

Soapwort makes an excellent rock garden plant. It is used for cleansing the skin for poison ivy rashes and other itchy conditions. It is especially useful in the textile industry.

CAUTION: Soapwort root is poisonous and should not be taken internally.

SOUTHERNWOOD

Artemisia abrotanum
Woody Perennial (fragrance, medicinal, ornamental)
Zones 4-8

HISTORY

Southernwood has a colorful history. It is also known as "lad's love," which is derived from being placed in lovers' bouquets as a a symbol of faithful affection even in bitter circumstances. Its history contains a number of "thought to's" such as: thought to be an aphrodisiac; thought to prevent baldness; thought to stimulate young men's passions; thought to stimulate hair growth; and thought to speed up facial hair growth. Even judges carried posies of southernwood and rue to protect them from the contagious diseases prisoners brought into their courts.

DESCRIPTION

Native to southern Europe, the French used southernwood for an insect repellent and knew it as *garde-robe* which was highly effective and could be counted on to drive insects away for up to eight months.

Valued first as an ornamental, southernwood is a member of the sunflower family and a relative of the wormwoods. It provides a gray-green feathery texture to the garden. Growing to 30 inches high and about 3 feet wide, it sometimes has very small yellow flowers which will appear in late summer. It is an evergreen and has a low spreading habit.

PLANTING AND PROPAGATION

Plant southernwood in average soil

that is well-drained and receives full sun. Divisions are usually taken in the spring or fall. Cuttings will also easily root. Space the plants at least 2 feet apart, since its stems reach out. Once southernwood becomes established, it is drought tolerant. It will take care of itself, but in order to keep it looking full, prune each spring to encourage it to grow upwards and not reach out.

HARVESTING AND STORAGE

Harvest the leaves of southernwood at any time, but for drying branches, pick just prior to flowering. Tie branches together and hang upside down.

USES

Tea can be made from the leaves and it is used medicinally as a stimulant, astringent and antiseptic. Use fresh branches in floral arrangements, wreaths, tussie-mussies and potpourri. Use dried branches in baths, floral arrangements, wreaths and as an insect repellent.

Southernwood makes a beautiful addition to a gray garden.

The branches are useful in making a yellow dye for wool.

SWEET CICELY

Myrrhis odorata
Perennial (culinary, ornamental, tea)
Zones 3-7

HISTORY

Also known as myrrh, sweet cicely is a member of the parsley family and native to Europe, but has naturalized in North America. It is commonly found in hedgerows and hilly areas and grassy places. In the 17th century, sweet cicely found favor in England and quickly became a favorite cottage-garden herb because of its sweet smelling, sugary leaves.

DESCRIPTION

Sweet cicely is the first to show in the spring and last to die down in the autumn. Growing as tall as 5 feet, cicely is a delicate herb with tiny white umbrella-like flowers which appear in May and blooms into June. Its leaves are ferny and the stem is very stout, hairy and grooved. It self sows freely so it has the potential to becoming invasive.

PLANTING AND PROPAGATION

In the early spring, sow seed very shallowly in a moist soil and light shade. Be aware the seeds are slow germinators. Storing the seed in the refrigerator may trick them into believing they have been through cold weather and germinate a little faster. The self-sown seedlings can be transplanted to the location desired. Propagate by root division in the autumn.

HARVESTING AND STORAGE

During the summer, leaves can be picked for using fresh since leaves do not dry well. The seedheads can be harvested just before turning brown. To experience their nutty flavor, the seeds can be eaten raw. To dry the seedheads, place in a paper bag and hang upside down so the seeds will fall into the bag. All parts of sweet cicely are edible.

USES

All parts can be used and with its strong anise scent, the foliage can be added to salads or cooked with fruits. Try it with rhubarb to reduce acidity and the need to add more sugar. This is a particularly useful herb for diabetics when using it to reduce sugar being added to foods.

The seeds of sweet cicely can be substituted for caraway seeds. Use those seeds to make tea. The leaves can be useful when making pastry, omelettes, soups, stews and even apple pie.

SWEET WOODRUFF

Galium odoratum & Asperula odorata
Perennial (dye, fragrance, ornamental)
Zones 3-9

HISTORY

Referring to the arrangement and texture of its leaves, "ruff" comes from *rovelle*, the French word for wheel. The prefix "wood" is a reference to growing wild in woods areas. Due to its fresh, hay-like fragrance, it was an important strewing herb and mattress stuffing in medieval times. Fresh woodruff leaves were used to staunch the flow of blood and cover wounds during the Middle Ages. It was also considered an important medicine for heart, liver and stomach problems. The Elizabethans made tussie-mussies from sweet woodruff flowers, which signified humility in the language of flowers, since it grows so shyly and close to the ground.

Even today, in parts of Germany, woodruff, with a little brandy and sugar is a flavoring for Rhine wine and drunk on the 1st of May. This is a traditional drink known as the "May bowl" and has been served to welcome spring since the 13th century.

DESCRIPTION

A member of the madder family, sweet woodruff grows to a height of about 6 to 8 inches. It is a long-lived spreading perennial and is evergreen in the South, but the top dies back when growing in the North. Tiny, white flowers create a carpet of stars in late spring and early summer.

It is native to Europe, Asia and North Africa becoming naturalized in other areas. It is cultivated in the United States. It is found in hedgerows and woods areas growing in loamy soil. The plant lacks fragrance when fresh, but when dried smells like new mown hay. It has erect, smooth, slender stems up to 10 inches with whorls of 6 to 9 dark green leaves looking much like the spokes of a wheel. The small, white starry flowers bloom in early summer followed by bristly seed balls.

PLANTING AND PROPAGATION

When planting seed, it is very slow to germinate and could take as long as 200 days. It probably would be quicker to purchase your first plants. They will then spread by means of underground stems and make a beautiful groundcover. May to June is its flowering period. It will tolerate dry soil only to a point. Shear in midsummer to promote denser growth.

Sow the seed in autumn in a moist, well-drained, rich soil in the shade if you are

prepared for a wait.

HARVESTING AND STORAGE

Pick fresh sweet woodruff when needed. Cut the entire stems when they are in bloom and hang to dry. The leaves and stems also freeze well.

USES

Use the fresh leaves in wine punches. It is delicious in most cold and fruit drinks, and fresh or dry leaves make a soothing tea. Steep fresh woodruff in white wine for a subtle vanilla flavor.

Use the dried leaves in potpourris, sachets and wreaths. It makes a beautiful ground cover.

The leaves produce a tan-colored dye and the roots will produce a red dye.

TANSY

Tanacetum vulgare
Perennial (dye, ornamental)
Zones 4-8

HISTORY

Tansy is native to Europe and Asia, but has naturalized in other areas. Found in hedgerows, along roadsides and on waste ground in northern parts of America its name is taken from the Greek word *athanasia*, meaning immortality. Because the flowers last so long and will not wilt easily, the name immortality became associated with tansy.

In Elizabethan times it was used to strew about the home to repel ants and flies.

It is still not unusual to see tansy hanging in doorways to deter flies. It was used to preserve meats and at one time tansy cakes were awarded to winning athletes. At one time sprigs of tansy were laid across corpses to preserve them from decay. Some say that tansy's strong smell was a relief during funeral rites in an era without air conditioning.

Today it is considered dangerous to eat and is grown strictly as an ornamental for a good source of cut and dried flowers for herb crafts.

DESCRIPTION

If you want an easy to care for plant, tansy is a drought tolerant perennial that is cheerful with its bright yellow, button-shaped flowers and lush, fernlike foliage. It is a member of the sunflower family and has a camphor pine-like scent. It will die down each winter and spring forth again in the early spring. Tansy can grow 3 to 4 feet tall and spread to 2 feet wide. Its blooming period is from July to September.

PLANTING AND PROPAGATION

Plant tansy in full sun to partial shade in well-drained average to poor soil. The richer the soil, the lusher the plant. Sow seed in the garden in spring or fall or begin plants inside in late winter and transplant outdoors 4 feet apart after danger of frost.

Divisions can be made in spring or fall. Tansy spreads by underground rhizomes and needs to be divided frequently, as it spreads widely. Pruning vigorously in mid-summer will produce lush growth in late fall.

Tansy foliage can be collected anytime during the summer and hung in bunches to dry. Flowers dry well but tend to lose their bright yellow color and become a little dull.

USES

The leaves and flowers are used to make a green-gold dye. The rhizomes make a green dye and the leaves a golden yellow dye.

Use the flowers in dried arrangements or in your fresh arrangements.

Tansy will repel insects, so it is wise to plant near fruit trees, put dried sprigs under carpets, or sprinkle in areas where you have trouble with ants and mice.

It's a good addition to your compost heap with its potassium content.

CAUTION: *Tansy is considered toxic and should not be taken internally.*

TARRAGON, FRENCH

Artemisia dracunculus
Perennial (culinary)
Zones 4-8

HISTORY

Native to Europe and Asia, its name comes from the French word *esdragon*, meaning little dragon. Because the roots of tarragon coil and entangle amongst themselves much as a dragon or snake's body does, the name little dragon applied.

In the Middle Ages, it was purported to prevent fatigue and when folks travelled by foot, they placed sprigs in their shoes. Thomas Jefferson helped by distributing the plants, as gifts, to dignitaries and colonists with whom he came into contact.

DESCRIPTION

Growing 2 to 3 feet tall, with a wide-spreading root system which can be invasive, tarragon is of two types: French tarragon, which is used for cooking, and Russian (*A. dracunculoides*), a much hardier variety, which lacks the flavor and aroma desired for cooking.

The Russian variety is much more invasive than the French. It is highly susceptible to wind and should be planted in a protected area.

The French tarragon should be treated as an annual where winters are cold. A member of the sunflower family, it has dark-green, small, pointed leaves all along its slender stems. It is not as invasive as the Russian and is most pleasant to have in the garden.

Mainly used for cooking, with its anise-like flavor, French tarragon is a natural accompaniment to fish and vinegar. White wine vinegar, in which its leaves have been steeped, is an important part of béarnaise sauce. French chefs could not, and would not, cook without tarragon. The leaves contain a strong oil and will easily dominate a dish if not used cautiously.

PLANTING AND PROPAGATION

Since the seeds of French tarragon are sterile, plant divisions of the root, or cuttings, which will take hold easily in the spring. Partial shade is tolerated, but full

sun is preferred. Plant in a well-drained, moderately-rich soil.

For protection, in the late fall remove the tops of the plant and build mounds up around the tarragon roots with sand, straw, or pine boughs, which can be discarded in the spring after all danger of frosts and some new growth has appeared.

The roots should be divided every 3 years in order to keep the flavor from deteriorating.

HARVESTING AND STORAGE

Harvest leaves of tarragon before the plants start to flower. Fresh tarragon is best; however, drying and freezing are good methods of preserving this herb. The leaves can also be preserved in oil or vinegar.

USES

Tarragon is the primary ingredient in béarnaise sauce and *fines herbes*. It is also used in many pickle recipes. Use it in egg dishes, cheese dishes, herbal butters, vinegar, and with fish, meats and tomatoes. Place a sprig of tarragon beneath the skin of your next baked chicken. Add tarragon to cream sauce or your next loaf of herb bread. It works equally well with vegetable dishes and enhances the flavor of parsley, chervil, garlic and chives.

THYME

Thymus vulgaris
Perennial (aromatic, cosmetic, culinary, medicinal, ornamental)
Zones 5-9

HISTORY

In medieval history, one of the best compliments you could receive was "you smell of thyme." The Greeks believed thyme, which is native to the Mediterranean, generated strength, so symbols of thyme were carried into battle to bolster courage. This could be the origin of the name "thyme" since *thymus* was Greek for courage.

Gardeners once planted beds of thyme, believing them to be homes to fairies.

Growing wild in the Catskill Mountains of New York, the seeds are said to have been brought into this area in the fleece of sheep shipped from Greece.

DESCRIPTION

A member of the mint family, thyme is a shrubby perennial with a pungent, clove-like aroma. The two types of thyme are creeeping thyme and upright thyme.

The creeping thymes, such as mother-of-thyme or wooly thyme, are low-growing. They are commonly found planted in walkways, where their aroma is released when stepped upon. Creeping thymes are perfect for rock gardens, since they love to creep around obstacles.

The upright types are more commonly used in the kitchen. Garden thyme (*Thymus vulgaris*) is a very popular cooking herb. It is a perennial evergreen plant growing to a height of about 12 inches, with narrow, gray-green leaves and pinkish flowers.

PLANTING AND PROPAGATION

Plant thyme in full sun in a light, well-drained soil. Seeds can be sown in the early spring after danger of frosts. Or, if you

prefer, transplants can be obtained from the nursery. Even though some varieties are hardy, they survive much better and get a faster start if they have received some protection through the winter. The creeping varieties have a longer life than the uprights, which should be replaced in 3 to 4 years.

Propagation can be by seed or stem layering. Because plants are so tiny to handle, seeds are best planted directly in an area of the garden where they are to remain. New plants are more quickly established by layering. To layer, use a wire hairpin to encircle the stem and push the pin into the soil. As soon as new roots appear and have taken hold, the hairpin can be removed and the root connecting it to the adult plant can then be snipped, creating a separate plant.

HARVESTING AND STORAGE

Leaves can be harvested anytime, but the best time is up to and through flowering. To keep thyme from becoming leggy clip it back soon after the flowers fade.

Thyme usually remains green during most of the winter, so your storage options are varied. The leaves can be dried and stripped from the stem or stored on the stem, since some recipes call for "sprig of thyme." The sprigs can be frozen and used as needed. After stripping the dried leaves from the stems, save the stems to throw onto the coals of your next cook-out.

USES

Thyme is one of the basic herbs in *bouquet garni* and is particularly good used in stuffings. Thyme improves many dishes and can be added in the early stages of cook-ing. Use it in soups, butters, and with meats, seafoods, and especially shellfish. Thyme serves as a substitute for salt.

It can be included in potpourri, especially the lemon thyme with its wonderful citric smell. Thyme makes a perfect houseplant since frequent cutting, for cooking purposes, will keep it thick and bushy.

Its medicinal uses include mouthwashes, and thyme pillows for relieving melancholy. Its oils were used as an antiseptic during World War I. It has been used as an antispasmodic for treating whooping cough and asthma. It contains oils which are soothing to skin pores. Poultices made from thyme were also used to treat headeaches.

VIOLET

Viola odorata
Hardy Perennial (aromatic, culinary, ornamental)
Zones 5-8

HISTORY

Some believe the word 'violet' comes from the Latin, *vias*, meaning wayside where violets are known to grow wild. Legend says the Greek god, Jupiter, grew violets to feed the goddess, Io.

Violets, a symbol of ancient Athens, were thought to spring up wherever Orpheus stepped. The Greeks and Romans found violets were a good substitute for honey and used it as a cough remedy. The blossoms contain 3 times as much vitamin C as oranges.

The violet was a token of love between Napoleon and Josephine and was later his emblem.

Historically it was used to cure epilepsy and help relieve depression. It is associated with reducing anger and as a sleep aid. In France, even today, violets are used to treat hangovers with their cooling nature. In treating migraines, where the head feels hot, cold compresses of violets can be applied directly to the head.

DESCRIPTION

Violets have dark green, heart-shaped downy leaves growing in thick clumps. They produce small, fragrant flowers which are white, pink, yellow or violet. They bloom with the tulips in April and into May. The flowers sport a lower petal resembling a spur and four upper petals in pairs. The plant grows no more than 12 inches high, depending on the variety.

Many species are common, such as pansies and Johnny-jump-ups. In the more than 500 *Viola* species, *viola odorata* is one of the more fragrant.

There is almost no maintenance associated with the violet. No need to fertilize. Simply leave them alone and they will flourish and spread rapidly.

PLANTING AND PROPAGATION

This herb is entirely self-pollinating and needs little help from us. The plant's blossoms are followed by closed flowers in the summer which bear capsules and eventually burst open to scatter their seeds. Plant in low sun or partial shade in rich, humus soil which is moist but well-drained. In very hot climates, shield from the afternoon sun.

Sow seeds very shallowly outdoors in the fall. Keep covered with burlap. In the winter or early spring, divide mature plants or detach runners which root every 3 to 5 inches. For a heavier bloom, fertilize in early spring prior to flowering.

HARVESTING AND STORAGE

The flowers can be picked at any time the plant is blooming. Dry flowers thoroughly for culinary use later and store in airtight containers. Violets can be used fresh or dried.

Remember, with violets, the more you pick, the more they bloom.

USES

Violets are a natural for window boxes. They make wonderful additions to nosegays. Use them to scent linens and colognes.

Petals or flowers may be candied to decorate cakes and petit fours or added to jams, puddings or fruit salads. Brush with egg white that has been beaten until frothy and sprinkle with superfine sugar. Allow to dry on waxed paper for 2 days and store in a closed container. These will keep for up to a year.

Add fresh flowers to salads, use to flavor honey, or garnish cream soups. Make a soothing tea. Float the flowers in punches and chilled white wines. For future use, flowers can be frozen in ice cubes for drinks.

YARROW

Achillea species
Perennial (dye, medicinal, ornamental)
Zones 3-8

HISTORY

Native to Europe and naturalized in North America, yarrow is common in pastures on embankments, roadsides and waste ground. The word, *achillea*, was most probably named after Achilles, who supposedly staunched the wounds of his soldiers on the battlefield with yarrow leaves. Its astringency helps to stem the flow of blood. It was still being used during the American Civil War.

DESCRIPTION

Wild or common yarrow (*Achillea millefolium*) is probably the most familiar yarrow, with its erect, rough, angular stem which reaches 3 to 4 feet high. It has attractive, feathery foliage that clasps the stem towards the top. Leaves and stems are covered in fine white hairs. Small daisy-like flowers bloom in flat top clusters which appear in late May or early June and will bloom through the summer. The flowers are usually white but may be tinged with pink. Yarrow is commonly thought of as a weed, but all herbalists welcome this "weed" in their gardens.

Fern-leaf yarrow (*Achillea filipendulina*) has a fern-like foliage on which yellow blooms appear in late May or early June and last about a month. Keep old flowers cut and the blooming period will be extended.

PLANTING AND PROPAGATION

Plant yarrow in full sun with an average, light, well-drained soil. When siting this plant, consider its height of possibly 4 feet and position near the back of the garden bed. It makes a nice backing to shorter plants. Yarrow needs a winter in the ground before blooming, so don't be surprised or disappointed if it does not bloom the first year.

Yarrow self-seeds freely. These plants can be transplanted where you would like them. You can also propagate by division or with seed in late spring.

Keep the plants deadheaded all summer to promote continuous flowering. In the fall, cut back to the ground.

HARVESTING AND STORAGE

When the flowers are completely open, cut and hang upside down in a dry, dark place. In 3-4 weeks you will be able to arrange for a beautiful golden bouquet or make a lavish wreath. The foliage of yarrow is aromatic and can be dried and used in potpourris and moth repellents.

USES

The flowers make a yellow or olive-colored dye. Or use your dried plants in flower arrangements or wreaths. Yarrow can be included in your moth repellent mixtures or in potpourris.

YUCCA

Y. filamentosa & Yucca spp. Liliaceae
Perennial (culinary, medicinal, ornamental)
Zones 4-10

HISTORY

Related to the lily family and found in the southwestern United States and Latin American countries, the yucca has naturalized in most areas of the United States. Its origination is thought to have been the West Indies. Yucca is known by many names. It's called desert candle, Spanish bayonet, and Adam's needle. The Native Americans used this plant for medicinal purposes, one of which was for aching joints.

DESCRIPTION

The yucca is well known for its stiff, sword-shaped leaves with sharp points and the white flowers that form in a single cluster atop a 4-to-6-feet tall stalk which rises from the middle of the leaves. The blooming period is July through August. Yucca needs to be planted in full sun and sandy, dry soil. It easily adapts itself to the incorporation of xeriscaping in your garden. Yucca, an evergreen plant, performs well and will add a nice vertical line in flower beds.

Mound lily yucca (*yucca gloriosa*) is naturalized from Florida to as far north as Zone 4. With its droopy habit and dark green leaves, it makes a great alternative to the Spanich bayonet and its dangerous pointy leaves.

PLANTING AND PROPAGATION

Spreading occurs when suckers at the base of the plant form and send up new leaves. Leaves can be as long as 2½ feet. When flowering is complete, it forms black capsule fruits.

Transplanting of parts of the root works well, but transplanting the entire plant works even better if you can find a very young plant and carry with it a large amount of soil. The parent plant resents being moved. Young offsets from the parent plant will transplant well. Plant at least 18 inches apart to allow for growth.

HARVESTING AND STORAGE

Maintenance of this plant will take only a little time as the dead leaves from the bottom of the plant need to be removed to keep a cleaner and neater appearance. This will not harm the plant as new leaves are forming at all times.

USES

The parts used in the yucca are the root and leaves. The white flower petals and the ripe pulp of the oblong fruits are edible and can be eaten raw or cooked. Its root is cooked much like a sweet potato. The leaves are extremely strong and used for basket making. The yucca has been used for arthritis and rheumatic pains.

PLANT HARDINESS ZONE MAP

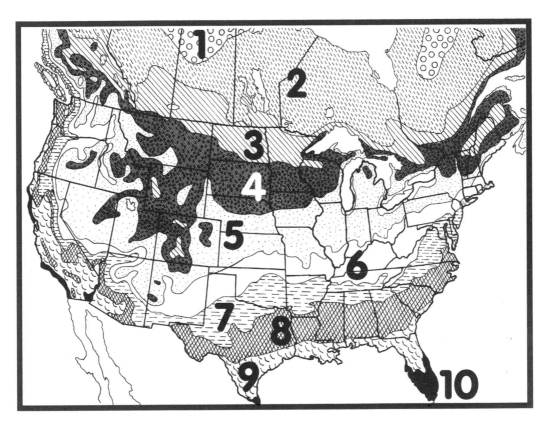

Average Annual Minimum Temperatures for Each Zone
— USDA —

Zone 1	below -50°F	Zone 6	0° to 10°
Zone 2	-40° to -50°	Zone 7	10° to 0°
Zone 3	-30° to -40°	Zone 8	20° to 10°
Zone 4	-20° to -30°	Zone 9	30° to 20°
Zone 5	-10° to -20°	Zone 10	40° to 30°

DESCRIPTIONS & USES OF HERBS

Angelica
Angelica archangelica
- flavor is sweet and licorice-like
- candy leaf stems; fresh or dried leaves in salads, soups, fish, poultry; seeds and dried root in tea, seeds and leaves in potpourri and air freshners; relieves travel sickness; foliage in floral arrangements

Anise
Pimpinella anisum
- sweet and aromatic with a distinctive licorice flavor
- fresh leaves in salads, fish, vegetables, mild cheeses, sweet fruits, yams; seeds in breads, cakes, candies, sachets

Basil
Ocimum Basilicum
- peppery, clove-like scent and a sweet taste
- fresh leaves in tomato-based dishes, sauces, soft cheeses, lasagna, spaghetti, salads, meats, baked fruits; sprigs or flowers as garnish; fresh or dried in eggs, beans, poultry, rice, fish, vegetables; add to butters, vinegars; floral arrangements; dried leaves in sachets, potpourri

Bay, Sweet
Laurus nobilis
- pungent but bitter taste
- flavor soups, stews, roasting game, meats, poultry; potato soup, vinegar, and when grilling fish; in marinades, salad dressings; repel storage pests; wreaths, dye making

Bee Balm
Monarda didyma
- strong rich, orangy fragrance
- floral arrangements and wreaths; fresh or dried leaves in tea and potpourris; a substitute for sage

Borage
Borago officinalis
- has a distinct cucumber taste
- salads and as a garnish; candy flowers to decorate cakes and cookies; vinaigrettes; good companion plant to strawberries

Calendula
Calendula officinalis
- petals as substitue for saffron in color only, not flavor
- petals for saffron in rice, potpourris, skin preparations; petals in wine punches, cheeses, salads, soups; bath water and floral arrangements

Caraway
Carum carvi
- taste is similar to parsley
- fresh leaves in salads; seeds in breads, cakes, soups and stews; chew leaf to cleanse breath; cook in sauerkraut, potatoes and cakes, beef, cheeses and fish; use root as you would parsnip

Catmint/ Catnip
Nepeta cataria
- mild, lemony mint flavor
- candy the leaves; use in tea and as stuffing for cat toys

Chamomile
Chamaemelum nobile (Roman)
- fresh apple aroma
- make chamomile tea; as a hair rinse or in potpourri; in bathwater to relieve sunburn

Chervil
Anthriscus cerefolium
- tastes similar to Italian parsley with hint of anise
- an ingredient in fines herbes; in vinaigrettes; add to butter or sauce to accompany fish or chicken; substitute for Italian parsley

Chives
Allium schoenoprasum
- has mild, sweet onion taste
- in any dish calling for onions; as a garnish for vegetables or soups; ornamentally in your garden; helps to prevent black spot on roses and repels carrot flies around carrots

Coneflower
Echinacea angustifolia
- vigorous perennial with dark green foliage, striking flowers
- bees, butterflies love this plant; a cut flower or use seedhead in crafts or leave in the garden to reseed and attract birds during winter months

Coriander (Cilantro)
Coriandrum sativum
- leaves have lemony taste to love or hate while seeds take on a spicy, orange fragrance
- fresh leaves in salads, salsas; with fish and poultry; seeds in cooked fruit and in curries; add to potpourri

Dill
Anethum graveolens
- spicy, anise-flavored leaves
- in soups, stews, fish sauces, and breads; with vegetables, making pickles; sprinkle on a salad or mix with cream cheese or sour cream for a dip; make dill vinegar; umbels in crafts

Fennel
Foeniculum vulgare
- a taste similar to licorice
- an appetite suppressor; flavor breads, cookies, soups, tomato sauces; toss in tuna salad; good substitute for breath fresheners

Feverfew
Chrysanthemum parthenium

- leaves strong, bitter scented
- leaves to lessen fat in food; flowers to potpourri for color and in fresh floral arrangements; greenish-yellow dye

Flax
Linum usitatissimum

- high in oils with linoleic acid
- basketweaving; fibers provide linen when spun; seeds used in breadmaking; in paint and varnish manufacturing and making linoleum

Garlic
Allium sativum

- taste strong and very pungent, but worth it
- medicinally, but mainly for cooking; in soups, butters, sauces and stuffings; when cooking meats, fish and poultry; add to herb vinegars; with tomato spread on French bread; companion plant to roses

Germander
Teucrium

- lightly aromatic
- in crafts; ornamental in the garden; use as hedges, borders or as a ground cover

Ginger
Zingiber officinale

- flavor is half spice, half citrus; a warm aroma; hot, biting taste
- in curry dishes or gingerbread; in tea, fruit salads, meats, poultry, pickles, sweet potatoes, carrots, rhubarb and peaches; with onions and garlic; when traveling to treat travel sickness

Horehound
Marrubium vulgare

- menthol-flavored
- make tea with leaves; used ornamentally and in floral arrangements

Horseradish
Armoracia rusticana

- root has a sharp, biting, pungent flavor
- a condiment to beef, seafood

Hyssop
Hyssopus officinalis

- hardy evergreen
- externally as poultice for bruising; in bathwater; border plant, crafts, floral arrangements

Lamb's Ears
Stachys byzantina

- retains silver-green color throughout the winter
- crafts and flower arrangements

Lavender
Lavandula

- a pleasing, fragrant scent
- in bathwater; leaves to flavor jellies, sugars and vinegars; in potpourri, sachets in linen storage; perfume soaps; floral arrangements; firelighters or skewers when grilling

Lemon Balm
Melissa officinalis

- strong scent of lemon
- cookies and cakes; tea, jellies and jams; add to potpourri; shine furniture

Lemongrass
Cymbopogon citratus

- lemon flavor, hint of ginger
- lemon tea; stir-fry foods, poultry, seafood; hair rinse

Lovage
Levisticum officinale

- very much like celery
- celery substitute to flavor salads, soups, stews, vegetables, meats, poultry, sauces; candy the stems

Marjoram
Origanum majorana

- sweet, spicy flavor, minty aftertaste
- salads, meats, fish, poultry, vegetables, Italian foods; flavor vinegars, soups, oil; fruit salads; bouquet garni; sachets, potpourri and bathing

Mint
Mentha

- cool, refreshing taste
- drinks, jams, jellies; with lamb, peas and potatoes; as a garnish; potpourri; breath freshner

Nasturtium
Tropaeolum majus

- soft, peppery taste
- petals to salads, butters, cream cheese; flavor oils, vinegars, dressings; garnishment

Oregano
Origanum

- strong heavy flavor
- ornamentally; vinegars, salads, Mexican, Italian dishes; in tomatoes, meats, cheese, fish, eggs and beans

Parsley
Petroselinum crispum

- curly variety, a pepper-like taste and the flat-leaf type has a richer, more robust flavor
- garnishment, odor-eater; insect repellent; most foods except sweets

Rosemary
Rosmarinus officinalis

- wonderful, sweet fragrance, bold flavor
- lamb, pork, fish or poultry; add to coals on your grill; butters, jams and jellies, vinegars

Rosemary (continued)
Rosemarinus officinalis
and breads; most vegetables and with most herbs; fruit dishes and drinks; hair rinse

Sage
Salvia officinalis
• lemony, camphor scent and slightly bitter
• fatty meats, stuffings with onions; sausage; pork, duck, cheese, tomato dishes; vegetables and fish; hair rinse for dark hair; room deodorizer; in crafts

Salad Burnet
Poterium Sanguisorba
• cucumber-like flavor
• substitute for cucumbers; in cream cheese, butters; garnishment; ornamentally

Savory
Satureja
• winter stronger than summer variety; spicy, peppery taste
• dried beans; add to vegetables; cheese dishes, eggs, meats, fish

Scented Geranium
Pelargonium
• highly scented
• jellies, puddings, sweets; teas, vinegars; cakes, barbecue sauces; sachets, potpourris, bathwater

Soapwort
Saponaria officinalis
• toxic if taken internally
• soap or shampoo; ornamentally; will relieve itchy skin

Southernwood
Artemisia abrotanum
• evergreen, musky fragrance
• floral arrangements; wreaths, tussie-mussies, potpourri; makes yellow dye

Sweet Cicely
Myrrhis odorata
• sweet smelling, sugary leaves
• salads, fruits; reducing sugar usage for diabetics; anise flavored tea; add to apple pie

Sweet Woodruff
Galium odoratum
• smells like new mown hay
• fresh leaves in wine punches, cold or fruit drinks; soothing tea; potpourris, sachets, wreaths; tan dye

Tansy
Tanacetum vulgare
• camphor, pine-like scent; toxic if taken internally
• greenish, golden dyes; fresh arrangements; insect repellent

Tarragon, French
Artemisia dracunculus
• aromatic anise-like flavor
• béarnaise sauce and fines herbes; egg and cheese dishes, butter, vinegar; fish, meats, and tomatoes and vegetables

Thyme
Thymus vulgaris
• strong, sharp taste with a clove-like aroma
• bouquet garni; stuffings, in soups, butters, meats, seafood; substitute for salt

Violet
Viola odorata
• dark green, heart-shaped leaves; fragrant flowers
• window boxes, nosegays; scent linens; candy the flowers or petals to decorate cakes; fresh flowers to salads; flavor honey, garnish cream soups; float flowers in punches, chilled white wines; freeze in ice cubes

Yarrow
Achillea species
• feathery foliage, daisy-like flowers
• olive-colored dye; fresh arrangements, wreaths; add to moth repellents

Yucca
Yucca filamentosa
• related to lily family; has stiff, sword-shaped leaves
• basket making

RECIPE INDEX